The Writer's Guide to

Crafting Stories for Children

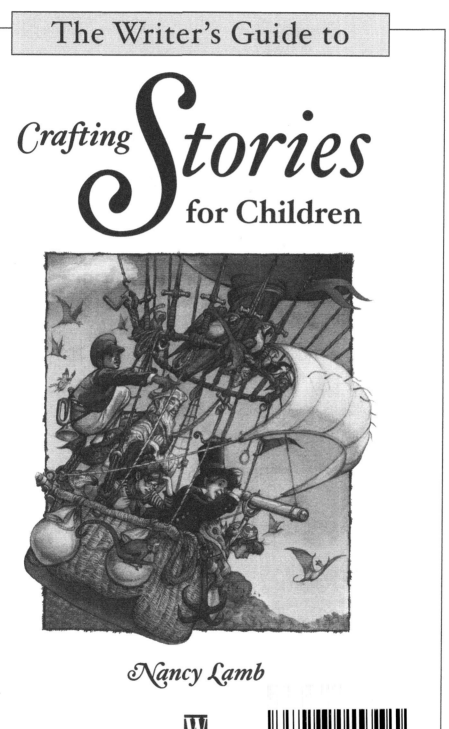

Nancy Lamb

WRITER'S DIGEST BOOKS
CINCINNATI, OHIO
www.writersdigest.com

D0191298

The Writer's Guide to Crafting Stories for Children. Copyright © 2001 by Nancy Lamb. Manufactured in the United States of America. All rights reserved. No part of this book may be reproduced in any form or by any electronic or mechanical means including information storage and retrieval systems without permission in writing from the publisher, except by a reviewer, who may quote brief passages in a review. Published by Writer's Digest Books, an imprint of F+W Publications, Inc., 4700 East Galbraith Road, Cincinnati, Ohio 45236. (800) 289-0963. First edition.

Visit our Web site at http://www.writersdigest.com for information on more resources for writers.

To receive a free weekly e-mail newsletter delivering tips and updates about writing and about Writer's Digest products, register directly at our Web site at http://newsletters.fwpublications.com.

18 17 16   17 16

Library of Congress Cataloging-in-Publication Data

Lamb, Nancy.
   The writer's guide to crafting stories for children / by Nancy Lamb.
     p. cm.
   Includes bibliographical references and index.
   ISBN-13: 978-1-58297-052-3 (alk. paper)
   ISBN-10: 1-58297-052-1 (alk. paper)
    1. Children's literature—Authorship. I. Title.

PN147.5 .L36 2001
808.06'83—dc21

2001033331
CIP

Edited by Michelle Howry and Donya Dickerson
Cover designed by Lisa Buchanan
Cover illustration by David Wenzel
Interior design by Joanna Detz
Production coordinated by Emily Gross

Praise for
The Writer's Guide to
Crafting Stories for Children

"So you want to write a children's book. Listen to Nancy Lamb. Your characters will come alive, your readers will become devoted. And your editors will love you."
—Constance Hale
author of *Sin and Syntax: How to Craft Wickedly Effective Prose*

"It's all here—everything you need to know about writing for children, presented with insight and humor. Nancy Lamb provides practical advice using classic stories as examples as well as her own twenty-five years of writing experience. Read it straight through like a novel (yes, it's that good) or use it as a reference book. A 'must have' for every novice or professional writer."
—Janet Zarem
children's book reviewer *Palisadian-Post*

"To be able to write for children is indeed a gift, but to be able to teach others to do it is an extraordinary talent. Nancy Lamb has the gift and the talent! Lamb, a master writer and storyteller, combines carefully chosen words with a dash of her wit and wonderful literary examples to create an indispensable recipe for anyone interested in writing for children."
—Laurie Sale
editor-in-chief FamilyEdge.com

"Nancy Lamb's book is much more educational than taking an entire semester of Children's Books 101 anywhere. I think it is the best book on the craft of writing for children that I have ever read as she covers every aspect of the art and craft of writing for kids in a detailed, informative and entertaining way. She doesn't miss a detail. Even established writers could learn a lot from this comprehensive guide."
—Andrea Brown
literary agent

Nancy Lamb Books and Other Credits

ADULT BOOKS

Fiction: *Gentlemen Callers*, 1978, Seaview Books; *The End of Summer*, 1981, Dell Publishing; *Dakin Field*, 1984, Pocket Books; *Prism*, 1988, Zebra Books

Nonfiction: *The Creative Revolution and the Future of Japan* (with Craig Brod, Ph.D.), 1994, Business-Sha (Tokyo)

CHILDREN'S BOOKS

Fiction: Which Way Books* ** (1980–1986, Simon and Schuster): *The Castle of No Return; Vampires, Spies and Alien Beings; The Spell of the Black Raven; Famous and Rich; Lost in a Strange Land; The Curse of the Sunken Treasure; Cosmic Encounters; Creatures of the Dark; Invasion of the Black Slime and Other Tales of Horror; Trapped in the Black Box; Poltergeists, Ghosts and Psychic Encounters; Islands of Terror Tenton Monster*

Secret Door Books* ** (1980–1984, Simon & Schuster): *Wow! You Can Fly!; Giants, Elves and Scary Monsters; The Haunted Castle; The Secret Life of Toys; The Visitor From Outer Space; The Inch-High Kid; The Magic Carpet; Happy Birthday to You; The Monster Family; Brontosaurus Moves In; The Enchanted Forest; Crazy Computers*

Rhyme and Reason (with Muff Singer), 1987, Price Stern Sloan; *The Great Mosquito, Bull and Coffin Caper*, 1992, Lothrop, Lee & Shepard, 1994, Beech Tree Books; *The World's Greatest Toe Show* (with Muff Singer), 1994, BridgeWater Books, 1995, Troll Books; *The Vampires Went Thataway!* (with Muff Singer), 1995, Troll Books

Nonfiction: *Vampires and Other Creatures of the Night* (with Rita Golden Gelman), 1991, Scholastic Books; *One April Morning: Children Remember the Oklahoma City Bombing*, 1996, Lothrop, Lee & Shepard

---

* (Written under the pseudonym R.G. Austin, with Rita Golden Gelman)
** (Some editions in Hebrew and Portuguese)

Dedication

To my friends and family members who, throughout my life, have offered me their wisdom and support. To the writers I have known who took the time to set aside their own work in order to critique mine. And to those other generous people I have encountered over the years who paused long enough in their busy lives to reach down and give me a boost up the ladder.

I am grateful to you all.

Acknowledgments

My thanks to Terry Baker, Joann Burch, Betsy James, Marianne Jas, Damon Kirsche, Michael Lippman, Mary Main, Andrew Martin and Susan Martin for their help, insight and suggestions as I wrote this book.

Thanks also to Andrea Brown, special agent.

My deepest, big-time, bended-knee gratitude to Janet Zarem—friend, book guru and reference goddess.

Nancy Lamb

The sky is bigger where I come from. When I was a child, I'd stand in the sun where the land was so flat and the horizon so far I could make out the curvature of the earth. That bright daytime vision did nothing to banish my nighttime terrors—the witch in my closet and the monster under my bed.

Whether I'm writing for adults or children, the war between my days and nights is reflected in my books. Although the tendency to acknowledge the light and dark sides of life is often disguised in my work, it's always there, lurking just out of sight in sly imitation of my demons of the dark.

Besides the power of the land and the menace of the monsters, my two sons, now grown, were the other major influence on my work. Since I wrote my first children's books for kids their same age, they served as blunt and humbling story consultants to a struggling writer.

Today I live near the ocean in Venice, California where I write and edit, work in the garden, play with my dog along the beach and spend time with friends. And when night comes, I never forget to close my closet doors.

❧

Nancy Lamb is the author of over forty books for children and adults, including *The World's Greatest Toe Show, The Vampires Went Thataway!, The Mosquito, Bull and Coffin Capter, Vampires and Other Creatures of the Night*, and *One April Morning*. She can be reached at her Web site, http://www.NancyLamb.com.

Table of Contents

PART ONE

Building
Plans

CHAPTER ONE

In the Beginning

Anybody who shifts gears when he writes for children
is likely to wind up stripping his gears.

—E.B. White

THE ART IN THE PROCESS

Most people think writing for children is easier than writing for adults. Just take a good story, simplify the plot, round the sharp edges, throw in a moral and use plain language. Thousands of writers turn out stories using this recipe. But these writers don't sell their stories to publishers. Children are sophisticated, savvy readers. They reject sermons. They avoid condescension. And they resent a dumbed-down attitude.

Storytelling is an art. And like any other art, it has rules. Picasso was trained in classical art before he became a cubist. In the beginning, he was taught to draw a bowl of grapes that looked like a bowl of grapes. Once he mastered perspective and line and shading, he could create any number of variations on that still life by juxtaposing the elements, turning around dimensions or stacking the third (unseen) dimension on top of the first. But even when he did so, he drew on the fundamentals of his classical training.

The same principle applies to crafting stories for children. Whether you're writing a traditional novel or an outasight, never-been-done, experimental book, the essence of storytelling remains the same. A good story flows from a solid understanding of writing and structure, along with a confident grasp of character and plot and dialogue. Once you've mastered the fundamentals, you can follow the rules, break the rules or create new ones. But whatever you do, you will always have a basic foundation to build on.

This book deals with fundamentals. We'll look at story ideas, style and structure. We'll explore what makes a character memorable and what makes the reader keep turning the pages. We'll talk about beginning, middle and end; about premise, theme and tone; about dialogue and point of view; conflict and structure; plot and subplot. We'll also talk about the importance of choosing a voice that enhances your story and the power of using the five senses to add texture and authenticity to that story. We'll examine how all these elements not only apply to children's literature but how they can apply to the creation of a viable and memorable children's book—a published book with your name on it.

THAT WAS THEN

Startled, you wake up in a cave on the side of a rugged ravine. The fading embers of the fire illuminate pictures of bear, bison and deer painted on rock walls that arch overhead. You hear an ominous growl. Red eyes glare at you in the dim light as you push your infant daughter behind you and grope for the spear. Your fingers tighten around the smooth oak shaft of the weapon. Moving into a crouching position, you find your balance and raise your arm. Suddenly, the massive shadow lunges toward you, and you hurl the spear. A wild shriek splits the silence of the dawn.

Later that morning, you huddle around a twig-fed fire seeking refuge from the dark of the night. Still shaking, you tell the story of the bear to the people gathered around you. You tell that tale from beginning to end, describing your fear and your miraculous escape from the jaws of a monster in breathless detail. For in ancient days, when life pulsed with magic and mystery, storytelling commanded a critical place in the life of a clan.

Four thousand years ago, *The Epic of Gilgamesh* mesmerized Babylonians. Almost three thousand years ago, Homer created the stories we call *The Iliad* and *The Odyssey*, capturing the imaginations of Greeks with tales of the Trojan War. In early eighth-century England, the exploits of Beowulf captivated the hearts and minds of Anglo-Saxons. In fact, the New Verse Translation of the story by Nobel Laureate Seamus Heaney has recently enchanted a twenty-first-century audience. The power of the oral tradition has given birth to *The Arabian Nights*, *Hamlet* and *Cinderella*. And it has celebrated the exploits of King Arthur and Captain Kidd, Pocahontas and Pancho Villa.

Stories that began as tales passed from one generation to the next were eventually recorded on clay tablets and papyrus, on vellum and paper— a priceless gift from our ancestors.

Throughout history, story has honored our past, enlightened our present and envisioned our future. Our forebears communicated knowledge, accumulated wisdom and commemorated common experience through the magic of words. They created myths and educated children. They also entertained crowds. Story has given birth to wars and provided the building blocks of peace. Story has forecast dangers, vilified enemies and celebrated heroes. Story has also illuminated our common humanity.

THIS IS NOW

Not much has changed in twenty thousand years. We still look to story for excitement, wisdom and comfort. And, I believe, we look to story for a connection to our past. Our ancient past. Story reaches beyond the written word to create an unconscious continuity with our earliest ancestors. And, in doing so, we honor where we came from, who we are and what we can become.

Helen Keller—blind, deaf and mute from the age of sixteen months— learned her first word when she was seven years old. Later, as an adult and noted educator, she described her wordless early world as "an unconscious but conscious time of nothingness . . . a dark, silent imprisonment. I did not know that I knew aught, or that I lived or acted or desired."

It is a privilege to write books. And it is especially a privilege to write books for children. Don't let anyone ever tell you that writing for children is a lesser art.

When you write a book for a child, you give him or her words—you give a voice to the voiceless. You open new worlds, introduce new ways of thinking and lift that child closer to the light. This is the power and purpose of story. And this is the gift the storyteller can give.

ART AND CRAFT

Some people are born with the gift of storytelling. You know them: friends who can talk about the most mundane encounter and capture your attention. They know just when to pause, when to draw out the details and when to deliver the punch line. They've got an instinct for story. Narrative comes naturally to them. Even if we're not among those fortunate few blessed with this inherent talent, most of us know a good story when we see or hear or read one.

Storytelling is not only a gift. It is an art. A craft.

Art involves instinct as well as an appreciation for form and structure. Most of us have that instinct. And if we don't, we can cultivate it.

Craft involves technique. Craft has rules. If a potter doesn't center the clay on the potter's wheel, he can't throw a pot. If a cabinetmaker doesn't measure the wood carefully, cut corners at the proper angle or join those corners correctly, she can't build a level table. What the potter and cabinetmaker produce may be art. But they could not produce that art without craft.

In craft, it's the process that matters.

That's what this book is about.

Process.

Chapter Two

Discovering Your Story

Good stories work on metaphoric and symbolic, as well as literal levels.
Children filter stories through their unique history and imagination,
using them in ways we can not possibly understand or even imagine.
Stories are food for the soul.

—*Frank Clancy*

INSPIRATIONS

I hear it all the time. "I've got these great stories. My children can't get enough of them. I'd love to put them in a book." Often such a statement is accompanied by an offer for me to write the stories. I tell the speaker in a gentle way that these bedtime treats belong to his imagination, not mine.

The fact is, we all have great stories in us.

Where do writers get their ideas? How do they pull their stories out of the ether and give them form? There is no special magic here, no right way to create stories, no single way to approach material. There are as many facets to a story as there are people to imagine it.

You may think you don't have enough good ideas for a viable children's book. But you're wrong. There are countless ways to generate ideas. You can reach into your own past or into the pasts of your grandparents. You can talk with friends, listen to conversations between kids on a playground, ask your own children what events in their childhoods have been most memorable, visit schools, reminisce with someone you meet on a plane, ask your elderly neighbor what it was like when she was an adolescent or look at photo albums of your own childhood to help recall the days when you were growing up.

Just as there are many ways to access stories, there are many ways to contribute to the care and feeding of our literary muse. We'll examine a variety of techniques to jump-start your story-telling engine. And we'll make sure you know how to keep that engine humming as you move from one book to the next.

REMEMBRANCE OF THINGS PAST

If we don't get seeds for our stories from something outside ourselves, we might recall incidents from our childhoods that inspire us.

That happened to me. One hot summer day when I was nine years old, my friend Patty was riding her bicycle and her barefoot brother was riding on the back of her bike. As Patty pedaled down the elm-covered street on her bicycle, her brother's foot brushed against the spokes of the wheel and—blech! you guessed it—the spokes cut off one of his toes.

As if this disaster weren't bad enough, at the same time her brother was being rushed to the hospital emergency room, Patty went in search of his severed toe. After scouring the leafy street, she not only found the toe, she saved it in a matchbox.

In no time at all, the toe turned black and wrinkled. Blessed with a generous nature, Patty made her wizened trophy available for our rapt inspection whenever we wished, doubling the preadolescent traffic in her house and elevating her status to neighborhood legend.

Most kids just looked at the toe. The brave kids touched it. Needless to say, Patty's parents were unaware of the cotton-wrapped treasure hidden under their daughter's bed, all of us understanding it would be best to deny the grown-ups knowledge of this particular secret.

Disgusting as this story might sound, my writing partner, Muff Singer, and I used this incident as the inspiration for our comic chapter book called *The World's Greatest Toe Show*—the opening line of which is, "The Canal Street Club wouldn't have caused so much trouble if Emily Anderson hadn't saved her father's toe in a matchbox."

Almost anything, no matter how outlandish, can be turned into a book. Everyone's childhood has incidents—comic or tragic, outrageous or ordinary—that contain the seeds of a first-rate story. Even a true-life tale of a severed toe. Finding a way to transform that incident into a story, as well as putting it into a viable form that kids will want to read, is both the challenge and the pleasure of writing.

THE MAGIC HOUR

Another place to find story ideas is in the Magic Hour. In the film business, the Magic Hour is what directors call the time before the sun sets. The light is soft, and the sun has a warm glow that flatters faces and makes scenes more visually appealing.

In the writing business, the Magic Hour falls at that time between sleeping and waking. The time when we drift without judgment, when unconscious thoughts bubble up to the surface without interruption from our conscious minds.

I get some ideas for stories when I'm in bed at night. But I'm usually so tired by the time my head hits the pillow I'm asleep before inspiration has the opportunity to knock on my story-dreaming door.

For me, a better time for creative thought is when I first awaken in the morning. Those floating moments between sleeping and waking invite me to drift, to let my mind wander over the tale I've been tossing around in my head or the character that's walked onto the stage of my imagination and refuses to disappear.

Whether it's at night, in the morning or in the middle of the day, we all experience our own renditions of the Magic Hour. The secret of writing well is not only to recognize that moment but to take advantage of it.

Opening Up to the Magic Hour

- Remember to breathe slowly and deeply. Breathe deep into your belly, yoga style, expanding both your chest and your belly as you inhale.

- Relax your entire body. Make sure your arms and legs are loose and your stomach is free of tension.

- Allow your mind to drift over your story. If you've got the seed of an idea, let it float free inside your imagination.

- Avoid waking up and being too alert. Dozing is all right.

- Drift. The object is to be open to random thoughts. Don't worry about making sense. Don't try to focus on anything specific.

- Put your internal judge in the closet. The goal is unimpeded access to your unconscious.

- Watch what floats into your mind. Make a conscious effort to put your thoughts on the back burner of your imagination where they continue to simmer as you go about your day.

- Keep a notepad nearby. Write down ideas that pop into your head, no matter how silly they seem.

THE CREATIVE NAP

In the early eighties when my partner, Rita Golden Gelman, and I were writing our pseudonymous series of Which Way and Secret Door books, Rita would fly into town, settle in my guest room, and we would get to work. For days on end, we'd write without a break.

The books we had contracted to write were "branching" books, print precursors of hyperlinked stories you see on Web sites today. The plotting was demanding and complicated. Each book for middle-grade readers had twenty or thirty primary plot lines and as many as forty endings. Constructing the stories—coming up with multiple plots and endless situations—was a task not made easier by the fact that we were writing on a typewriter and not a computer. We did have a system, however.

First we would lay out our central themes and plot points. Then I'd sit in front of the typewriter, close my eyes, take a few deep breaths and allow my imagination to do its work.

Indebted to that magic called the creative process, I'd spin out one tale after another. When I'd get stuck, I'd turn to Rita.

"What now?" I'd ask. "What does the hero do next?"

"How about if you have him find a buried treasure? Or, what if the pirates chase him into the cave?"

"That's it!" I'd say, turning back to the typewriter.

Day after day we produced one multiple-choice story after another. As soon as I wrote a page, I would hand it to Rita for her to rewrite, edit and organize. In spite of the fact that we were functioning as a well-oiled story machine, every afternoon around two or three o'clock I would become inordinately sleepy. This sinking spell usually coincided with the moment in my creative day when my well of ideas ran dry.

In the beginning I struggled to stay awake, calling on the standard arsenal of pick-me-up tricks: a quick walk, a cup of espresso or brisk Irish tea, a piece of dark chocolate. But no matter how hard I tried or how much coffee and chocolate I ingested, nothing worked. My bed was fifteen feet from my desk, and all I wanted to do was sleep. Finally I gave in to my craving.

Every afternoon I would tell Rita to wake me up in forty-five minutes, then I'd lie down, sack out and take advantage of the Magic Hour. Sometimes I slept. Sometimes I drifted. But always I would awaken refreshed and ready to turn out more pages.

The Quick Snooze

Work is an excellent excuse for dozing off in the middle of the day. Einstein, Edison and Churchill all believed in the power of the nap. And their creativity is the stuff of legends.

I'm happy to follow in the footsteps of the masters. In fact, I've gotten some of my best ideas during the Magic Hour when I lie down, close my eyes, and forget about all the things I have to do and all the errands I have to run. Even if it's for fifteen or twenty minutes, I've learned to profit from taking a nap.

Ever since writing the Which Way books, I've called on the services of the Quick Snooze whenever I'm stuck on a book or a story line or even a phrase. Sometimes I don't go so far as moving over to the bed to lie down. I put my feet on my desk, lean back in my chair and close my eyes. Ninety percent of the time, if I open myself up to possibility—if I don't try to make something happen, but allow it to happen—I find a solution.

The Creative Nap is a kissing cousin of meditation. For those of you who practice yoga or chi gong or meditate daily, you know how refreshing these exercises are. You probably also know how often you get ideas when you're in a meditative state.

Whatever method you use to shift into an open, receptive space, try to do it on a daily basis. Your creativity will flourish, and so will your writing.

The Stuff That Dreams Are Made Of

Everybody dreams. Grown-ups dream, and children dream. Dogs, rats and dolphins dream. Babies dream when they're still in their mother's wombs. And whales, lions and leopards dream, too. Even people who claim they don't have dreams dream.

In a moment of stunning insight just before the turn of the twentieth century, Sigmund Freud called dreams "the royal road to the unconscious." Long before Freud, Greeks, Romans and Egyptians conferred a special power and significance to dreams. So did Jacob and Moses.

Throughout history, the tales we spin in our sleep have occupied a place of magic and mystery and power in our waking lives. In spite of the fact that a few neurophysiologists and psychologists believe dreams are no more than random firings of brain activity during sleep—a form of nighttime neuronal calisthenics—contemporary studies indicate that dreams help us learn new things and lay down long-term memories.

Personally, I believe the function of dreams goes beyond this. When I'm working on a book or just thinking about stories, I often awaken in the middle of the night with an insight into a character or a solution to a plot problem. As a consequence, I'm not only willing to regard dreams and their sleep-drenched aftermath as a significant way to access ideas and inspirations percolating beneath the surface of my consciousness, but I welcome their presence into my creative life.

Capturing Dreams and Other Night Visions

The only time to capture a dream is immediately upon awakening. With the few exceptions of horrific nightmares and unusually vivid or recurring dreams, most dreams and nocturnal fancies evaporate within a minute or two of waking up. If we don't write them down immediately, they will be lost to us forever.

In order to glean all the benefits from our natural creative process, there are several ways to take advantage of dreams, night visions and other inspirations of the dark.

- Keep a notebook and pen by your bed. Use them. This practice is essential for any serious writer. If you have a sleeping partner or a roommate who would take unpleasant exception to your turning on the light at four in the morning, invest in a small flashlight.

- Do whatever it takes to write down the idea that comes to you in the middle of the night. Even if you think your idea is so creative and so inspired you couldn't *possibly* forget it, write it down anyway. I can guarantee that if you do not write it down, chances are you'll forget even the most brilliant and memorable idea. More than once I've awakened in the morning with the recollection that I had a fabulous idea in the sleep-drenched dark. But I was too tired to write it down, so I turned over and closed my eyes. *Hasta la vista, baby.*

- If you don't want to wake up enough to turn on the light, the least you can do is jot down the idea on an index card. A few jumbled words scribbled in the dark are better than no words at all.

If you're one of those people who doesn't recall dreams, try this: After you close your eyes at night, remind yourself to remember your dreams. Make a determined, conscious decision not to lose your dreams before they drift into the dark well of your unconscious. The moment you wake up—especially if you awaken suddenly from a dream—reach for your notebook and write it down. You'll be amazed at how your dream recollection improves.

A JOURNAL FOR YOUR JOURNEY

Not all writers keep a journal. But if you haven't done it thus far, I suggest you try it. Journals can be an invaluable source of inspiration for those times when you're slogging your way through a creative desert. They're also great reminders of where you have been and how far you've come. Whether you scribble in your journal every morning or make an entry once a week, the act of committing ideas to writing helps you gain insight into your actions and transform inspirations into reality.

I know a woman who created an entire novel from journal notes she made over a period of a year and a half.

"This was a profound and painful time in my life," she told me. "I thought I'd never forget it. But when I began to write my book, I was amazed at how much I'd forgotten. If it hadn't been for my journal, I would have lost all the small details and critical insights that lent authenticity to my story."

Journals help us capture the intensity of emotions while they're still fresh in our minds and remember details of events before they're eroded by the winds of time. Journals are containers of lists and calendars, thoughts and feelings, reminders and reminiscences. They help us face our demons and confront our ghosts. Journals feed us ideas and jumpstart our stories. They show us how to clear the path between consciousness and creativity. And they show us how to light the way between imagination and the written word.

Whatever your original reason for keeping a journal, chances are it will evolve into something more. If you haven't yet tried it, go out and buy yourself a book to write in. Anything will do. When it comes to recording thoughts, a spiral notebook is just as effective as a handtooled, leather-bound diary.

STRAW INTO GOLD

Just as Rumpelstiltskin spun straw into gold for the miller's daughter, our challenge as writers is to take the straw we find in our daily lives and weave it into stories that engage the imaginations of children.

I live near the ocean in Venice, California. Not long ago, I took my dog Max to a grassy area by the beach to play with his friend Dodger. It was past ten o'clock at night, and as the dogs romped together on the grass, a huge bird swooped overhead and flew across the bike path to the beach.

"What was *that*?" I asked Dodger's owner, Cliff.

"A gull?"

"Seagulls don't fly at night," I said.

"Pigeons, pelicans and crows don't, either," said Cliff. "And that bird was too large for a bat."

Our eyes followed the bird—visible in the dim light from the street lamps—as it landed on the post that secured one end of a beach volleyball net.

I walked onto the sand.

The bird didn't move.

I took at few steps closer. The bird stayed on the top of the post.

Astonished, I motioned to Cliff, who walked over and stood next to me.

Perched on the volleyball post as if he were waiting for the game to begin, a horned owl stared straight at us.

Cliff and I stood there for ten minutes looking at our unexpected night visitor. Finally, the owl tired of basking in the glow of our human awe. With a shrug, he spread his wings and flew into the dark toward the lifeguard station.

I don't need to tell you that seeing an owl at the beach is not just unusual, it's outright miraculous. Owls are not beach birds. They're nocturnal creatures that prefer woodlands to ocean. Furthermore, they are not given to hanging around areas where human beings can admire them in the middle of their nightly hunt. That is the only time in my life I have ever seen an owl that wasn't captured on film, stuffed by a taxidermist or trapped between the pages of a book.

Looking for Owls in Our Own Lives

The owl on the beach is an indelible example of the conjunction of the prosaic and the improbable. These two elements do not belong together, which is precisely what makes them memorable.

We all encounter the extraordinary in the ordinary; it happens all the time. But caught up in the demands of our daily lives, we often fail to take the time to see them, to envision them in a story or to open ourselves to the possibility of mystery.

Although I haven't used this owl incident in one of my books yet, it is faithfully recorded in my journal, which I drew on for this book. So there are lots of ways to use ideas—not the least of which is to expand our imaginations and help us remember.

Let's say you want to create a variation on the theme of the owl in a story of your own. You could begin a young adult (YA) novel with the appearance of the owl on the beach—a metaphor for a boy who feels out of place in his own environment. Or you could begin a picture book with the same image and a similar premise. In other unusual pairings, you could write a story about a girl who has a clam as a pet, or a boy who hand-feeds nectar to a wing-damaged butterfly throughout its month-long life span.

When you write, make it a point to seek out unusual combinations and unexpected relationships. Whether these conjunctions occur in your inner or your outer life, whether they're encountered in a daydream, a car full of kids, or a walk through the produce section at the grocery store, look for those things that fit together even when they don't seem to.

I once wrote a line in a poem that said, "I do not believe in guilt, moderation or dull pencils." These three things have nothing in common except the sensibility of the writer that connected them. That creative leap is the glue that binds unusual elements together—and the glue that can bind your story.

E.B. White's classic *Stuart Little*—the tale of the mouse that lives with a human family—is a brilliant example of combining the ordinary and extraordinary. This isn't a mere mouse that lives behind a hole in the wall and occasionally peeks at Johnny while he's eating breakfast. This is a mouse born and raised in a human family just like any other kid.

D. Manus Pinkwater's *Lizard Music*—a wildly original and comic middle-grade novel in which a lizard quintet plays a prominent role in the story—is another example of the conjunction of the prosaic and the outrageous.

The most popular children's book in decades takes an ordinary English boy named Harry Potter and sends him to wizard school. This particular blend of the commonplace and the fanciful has skyrocketed this series into the stratosphere in every corner of the globe.

❧

Whether you're combining words that have no obvious connection or elements that have no obvious relationship, the important thing is to welcome the outrageous, the fantastical and the unusual into your life. Whether these inventive concoctions occur in a reverie or on a walk in the woods, stay open to the wonder and receptive to the dream. That's when imagination takes the most improbable and memorable creative leaps. And that's where your story begins.

KEEPING THE FAITH

Before we move into how books are structured and written, I want to emphasize up front that there is no right or wrong way to write your book. There is no magic formula, no perfect way to approach your story. But there is the accumulated wisdom of thousands of years of storytelling and the collective experience of writers who have walked this path before you.

Ultimately, the best way to write a story is to find a strategy that works for you. Within this context, it's important to understand that there are lots of approaches to storytelling. I'll discuss many of these ideas in detail in the pages ahead. When you look for a way to tell your story, your most critical goal should be to find a method that fits your temperament, feeds your intellect, and gives you the courage to move forward with confidence and conviction.

Your Turn
Ideas to Get You Started

If you don't already have a journal, get yourself a notebook in which you can record your ideas, thoughts and feelings. Place this journal on your bedside table where you can reach for it first thing in the morning.

Even if writing in the journal feels awkward at first, set a goal of jotting down your thoughts for seven minutes every morning. If seven minutes seems too daunting, do it for three minutes or even two minutes. The object of the exercise is the daily discipline of the doing, not the sense and sensibility of the sentences.

Revving the Creative Engine

If you don't know what to write about, try setting an agenda the night before. Each night before you go to bed, write a topic across the top of a new page in your journal. This is the subject you'll begin to write about the next morning. Consider this topic a jumping-off point, not a classroom essay question. Don't make any rules for yourself beyond the simple act of writing. Forget spelling, grammar and punctuation. You can't flunk journal writing. Set your imagination free and see where it takes you. As they said in the hippie days of yore, "go with the flow."

If you can't think of anything to write about in the beginning, consider some of these topics.

- What was my favorite book when I was a child?
- What was my favorite book when I was a teenager?
- What made my childhood books special to me?
- What's the worst lie I ever told?
- What's the scariest thought I had as a child?
- What's the scariest thing that ever happened to me when I was a child?
- What's the scariest thing that ever happened to me as an adult?
- What was my greatest happiness as a child? Why?
- What was my greatest fear? Why?
- What does loss mean to me today?
- What did loss mean to me as a child?
- Where did my monsters live in the dark? In the closet? Under the bed? Behind the curtains?
- Who were my monsters in the dark?
- If I could control my dreams, what would I choose to dream about?
- What is the scariest dream I've ever had?
- What made me feel most secure as a child?
- What was the best school experience I ever had? What was the worst?
- How would I have reacted if my most secure anchors were removed from me when I was a child?
- What was my favorite age as a child?
- Who was my best friend when I was growing up? What was wonderful about him or her?
- If I could return to my childhood and take one thing with me that I've learned as an adult, what would that nugget of wisdom be and how would it change my life?
- How could I apply that lesson to a children's book?

CHAPTER THREE

From ABC to YA: An Overview

To talk to a child, to fascinate him, is much more difficult
than to win an electoral victory. But it is also more rewarding.

—Colette

WHAT AND HOW LONG?

Although opinions vary, there is a general consensus about how long different kinds of children's books should be and what they should contain.

There's always flexibility in the way you approach length and subject matter. However, if you think you want to try something different—if you want to write a one hundred-page picture book or a sixty-page YA novel—it's best to understand the parameters of the genre before you stray too far afield. Once you get a grasp on the logic behind the structure of established book formats, it might make more sense to follow the rules than to break them.

This chapter provides an overview of the different categories in children's literature, beginning with first books—ages one and up—and ending with YA books—ages twelve and up.

A CHILD'S FIRST BOOKS

Jim Trelease, the noted expert on the benefits of reading aloud to children, says that a child's first books should "provide joy." Books accomplish this by lending context and meaning to the things children see and experience.

First books come in all sizes, shapes and colors, and are an entity unto themselves. Since the following chapters of this book generally deal with books for older kids, I'll go into a bit more detail about first books in this chapter.

In these early books, there can be one word on the page or thirty words on a page. What matters is the young child's connection to the content of the book.

When my son was fourteen months old, he loved to cuddle on my lap with Richard Scarry's *Best Word Book Ever* spread out in front of him. He could sit for hours pointing to pictures on the page. Toothbrush, cup, ball. Cherry picker, pumper truck, hook and ladder. What joy he took in naming the objects he saw and finding the picture story on the page! And what pride he took in mastering his world through words.

First books are memorable because of the feelings they evoke in a child. These books pique interest and invite laughter. They engage minds, engender pride and encourage curiosity. Something as elaborate as a pop-up book or as simple as a piece of fuzzy fabric pasted on a picture of a kitten can capture a child's attention and imprint itself in memory for the rest of his life.

Although first books are generally simple, there are several qualities that elevate the best of them to classics, including the fact that the most notable books deal with universal themes. Loss, fear, love, anxiety, anger, loneliness, joy, curiosity, greed, humor. All the things that make us laugh and cry—the things that mark us as human. The more of these attributes you use in one book, the more effective that book will be.

Nine Ways to Enliven a Child's First Book

1) Present an Intriguing Situation. In *Hey, Kid!* by Rita Golden Gelman, a big kid convinces the hero to accept a large box with a mysterious surprise inside. The surprise is a charming monster who creates unwitting havoc in everyone's life. At the end of the book, the hero—exhausted from coping with the antics of the well-meaning but trouble-making monster—pawns off the mystery box on another unsuspecting child. The story comes full circle and is as amusing as it is creative.

2) Challenge the Imagination. In *Possum Come a-Knockin'* by Nancy Van

Laan, the story starts innocently enough with a possum knocking on a door. This single act triggers a series of raucous events inside the house, with each response from an additional family member becoming more outrageous than the last. As in:

> Then . . . Baby came a-crawlin'
> and dawg started howlin' . . .
> as Ma followed Pa to the door.

Needless to say, the naughty possum enjoys every moment of chaos his presence creates.

3) Embrace Humor. In *Slugs* by David Greenberg, the story begins with all the things you can do with slugs—everything from serving them for breakfast to launching them in rockets to sucking them through straws. The story ends with the revenge of the slugs—how they will come to you in the middle of the night and chop you into pancakes, butter you with germs or turn you inside out. Once again, bringing the story full circle creates the preposterous and satisfying humor in the book.

4) Play With Interesting Words. In Jack Prelutsky's *It's Raining Pigs and Noodles*, the author takes an obvious delight in playing with words, as in his short poem "The Otter and the Ocelot."

> The otter and the ocelot,
> As fortunate as they could be,
> Now sail the seas upon their yacht—
> They won the OCELOTTERY.

5) Use Repetitive Language. In *Sid and Sam* by Nola Buck, the author finds ways to repeat words, or variations of those words, in a delightful exercise in early reading.

"Sid," Sam said. "That song is so long." "So long?" said Sid. "So long," Sam said. "So long, Sid."

6) Invite Participation. In *A Puppy to Love* by Muff Singer, the book is designed so you pull a cuddly puppy out of the spine of the book.

The author asks the reader to show the dog how to do several activities, such as run fast, eat ice cream and play hide and seek. At the end of the book, the reader is invited to give the puppy a big hug and tuck him into bed. This is a perfect participatory experience for a small child.

7) Offer Visual Clues. In *Bookstore Cat* by Cindy Wheeler, Mulligan the cat spies a pigeon, and when he goes after it, he creates havoc. Every step of the story has an illustration that prompts the reader to continue offering visual clues to the words on the page. This blending of words and pictures is an ideal way to help a child learn to read.

8) Use Rhythm and Cadence. Sometimes this involves rhyme. Sometimes it doesn't.

In *Rain*, Manya Stojic uses a comforting, repetitive cadence to convey her gentle message.

> *The rain is coming!* . . .
> *The porcupine smelled it. The zebras saw it. The baboons heard it.*

9) Explore Universal Themes. Margaret Wise Brown's *The Runaway Bunny* is ostensibly a story about a little bunny who wants to explore new things. But it's also a story about separation and anxiety and the universal longing for security in the midst of a challenging world. These deeper themes elevate the story from the particular to the universal, making this book an enduring classic.

⌘

Whatever you decide to write about, however you decide to approach your subject, write your first books with these attributes in mind.

Don't be afraid to dig deep when writing books for this young age group. Stories for young children should present themes that create magic and mystery, that elevate a common experience into the realm of memorable. These are the elements that make the difference between an ordinary and an extraordinary reading experience for a child—the themes that illuminate a classic.

PICTURE BOOKS, AGES THREE–SIX AND FOUR–EIGHT

Most picture books are twenty-four or thirty-two pages long. Some, however, are forty-eight pages long and written for older readers. The best picture books, such as *Goodnight Moon* by Margaret Wise Brown, address universal themes and appeal to adults as well as children.

On the surface, *The Tale of Peter Rabbit* by Beatrix Potter is about naughty rabbits eating carrots in Mr. McGregor's garden. But as Eden Ross Lipson notes in her *New York Times* article, "Children generally grasp the fact that Beatrix Potter was writing about life and death."

My all-time personal favorite is Maurice Sendak's *Where the Wild Things Are*, a picture book so brilliant and so deceptively simple that of all the books written for children, I wish I could have written that one. This book presents an intriguing situation, challenges the imagination and embraces humor. It uses rhythm and cadence and repetition. It also invites participation and explores universal themes.

Although *Where the Wild Things Are* addresses the consequences of being naughty, it also digs deeper into a child's psyche. In acting out, Max, the hero, is forced to look at and deal with his anger, personified as monsters in the story. He not only confronts his monsters, he learns to tame them within the behavioral boundaries his mother has set—a critical life lesson for any child. Eventually Max comes to understand that his mother still loves him, even when he misbehaves.

Picture Story Books, Ages Three–Seven. Most picture story books are twenty-four to forty-eight pages long. The youngest books tell a simple story, one that often deals with how something works or how a problem is solved. Since picture story books are told in relatively few words, the plots are necessarily simple. The hero has a problem, confronts complications and discovers a solution.

In *What's Under My Bed?* James Stevenson's young heroes spend the night at their grandparents' house, where they hear a scary story before bedtime. This evokes all the monsters of the dark. When the kids tell their grandfather the next morning, the grandfather tells the children about *his* monsters, thus allaying the children's fears.

EASY READERS, AGES SEVEN–NINE

Most easy readers are 1,000 to 1,500 words long, or thirty-two to sixty-four pages. Some easy readers have chapters, and some don't. The subject of most of them is lighthearted, although a few deal with more serious issues. Easy readers are written for three different reading levels.

1) Preschool Through First Grade. These books have simple concepts and lots of repetition. They use large type with few words on a page. They also use visual clues to help the child figure out what a word might mean.

In *Toad on the Road* by Susan Schade and Jon Buller, the authors begin with, "I love to drive! I am a Toad. Here I come—Toad on the road!" As the Toad drives through town, he meets a cat, stops for lunch and gives a pig a ride in his car. By the end of the book, the car is jammed inside and out, and the reader has learned new words through repetition and rhyme.

2) First Through Third Grade. These books for the developing reader have slightly smaller type than the first level. The stories are more complex, but the sentences are short and simple, and the word choices are limited.

In *Eek! Stories to Make You Shriek*, Jane O'Connor offers three stories in one simple book. The shortness of the adventures and the creativity of the plot twists help children build confidence in their reading skills.

In O'Connor's story called "Halloween," Ted goes to a Halloween party and meets a strange monster he assumes is his friend Danny. Later, Ted learns that Danny was at home and sick in bed; he never went to the party. This leaves the hero wondering who that strange furry monster really was.

3) Second Through Third Grade. These books have more complicated plots and more complex sentences. The vocabulary is also more advanced. Still, they are simple stories.

In *Just a Few Words, Mr. Lincoln*, Jean Fritz tells the story of how Abraham Lincoln came to write the Gettysburg Address and how the President thought the speech was a failure after he delivered it. As it turns out, of course, the Gettysburg Address has become one of the most famous speeches in history.

Chapter Books, Ages Seven–Ten

Most chapter books are 1,500 to 15,000 words long or forty to eighty pages. These books, divided into eight to ten short chapters, are written for kids who can read and who can handle reasonably complicated plots and simple subplots. Chapter books occupy a special place in kids' hearts. This is the first time they are reading something that resembles a grown-up book.

Written with lots of dialogue, the vocabulary in chapter books is challenging, and words can often be understood by the context of the sentence. Most chapters are self-contained with a beginning, middle and end. But some chapters move the plot forward by means of cliffhanger endings.

In Patricia Reilly Giff's *The Secret at the Polk Street School*, the kids in Mr. Rooney's class want to win the banner for the class that makes the greatest contribution to the school. Dawn goes in search of a mystery and finds one when she assumes the role of the wolf in the class play. Told in ten chapters, the story captures the fun of childhood along with the complications and challenges of elementary school life.

MIDDLE-GRADE NOVELS, AGES NINE–TWELVE

Most middle-grade novels are 15,000 to 35,000 words long or 64 to 150 pages. These books have a wide vocabulary. They have a plot and a subplot and are often comic, but can also deal with serious subjects. The chapters usually have cliffhanger endings and the emphasis in most of these books is on character.

In *Fourth Grade Rats*, Jerry Spinelli tells the story of Suds, a boy who used to be a good kid. But in fourth grade, his friend Joey teaches him, it's important to be a rat—the next step to being a man. In his efforts to fit in and be tough, Suds learns a hard lesson about the consequences of his actions and the choices he makes.

YOUNG ADULT (YA) NOVELS, AGES TWELVE AND UP

Most YA novels are over 30,000 words long or 120-250 pages. Although younger YA novels can deal with intense and serious subjects, they are often mysteries and thrillers—stories engrossing enough to appeal to younger kids as well as older ones. The older YAs deal with more complex subjects.

What distinguishes a young adult novel from an adult novel is often nothing more than subject matter. These books are complicated, sophisticated and challenging. They are not limited in what issues can be discussed, nor are they in any way "kids' books." By this age level, there is a high tolerance for ambivalence in both character and plot, as well as a general acceptance of complex and painful subjects.

In *Give a Boy a Gun,* author Todd Strasser deals with the tragic aftermath of the chaos created when two boys use semiautomatic weapons and homemade bombs to storm a school dance. The story is told from multiple points of view, presenting insights and opinions from both students and administrators about everything from gun control to bullying to peer pressure.

In *Dancing on the Edge,* Han Nolan takes on the subject of how our pasts color our present lives. In a complex and demanding, funny and tragic story, Miracle McCloy is constantly reminded that she was born by being rescued from the womb of her dead mother. A series of incidents in her life causes Miracle to examine the reality in which she lives. Shocked by the loss of her sense of self, she eventually ends up in a psychiatric hospital where she must learn to trust her feelings as well as the intentions of the people who love her. This is a good example of a demanding subject treated in a sophisticated way.

To Be or Not to Be Literary

Occasionally beginning writers ask about what kind of book they should write. Should they write a commercial book geared to the mass market—those thrillers and adventures such as the Goosebumps and Finnegan Zwake series that kids consume like popcorn? Or should they aim for a more literary market, with books such as *The Giver, A Wrinkle in Time* and *Where the Red Fern Grows?*

My advice about the commercial vs. literary debate is short and simple: Don't worry about it. Produce the best story you can. Write it, craft it, rewrite it, hone it, edit it and love it. When you're finished, the publisher will decide what kind of book it is.

PART TWO

Foundation
& Structure

CHAPTER FOUR

Structural Design

Structure is nothing more than a way of looking at your story material so that it's organized in a way that's both logical and dramatic.

—*Jack M. Bickham*, Scene & Structure

FUNDAMENTAL STRUCTURE

Structure isn't a prefabricated box you cram your story into. It is a flexible framework that helps you move through your narrative without losing your way.

Think of structure as a series of road signs posted along the journey of your story. Think also of structure as the rails that keep you from straying onto the meandering paths that can so often lure a writer from the true course of a story.

Structure creates the underpinning of a book. Without it, narrative has no form and plot has no provocative way to move the reader from one moment to the next or from one scene to the next.

The most basic element of structure is what we were all taught in school: beginning, middle and end. If there is a fixed star in the universe of storytelling, this is it. Every story has a beginning, middle and end. Every scene has a beginning, middle and end. But how these elements are dramatized—how they are conceived and shaped, juxtaposed and presented to a reader—is up to you.

Just because storytelling has rules, this does not mean your creativity will be crammed into a premeasured, preset box. What this does mean is that a basic understanding of structure frees you to do your job as a creative writer. Think of Picasso and that bowl of grapes from chapter one.

As I said earlier, there is no one perfect way to fit the puzzle pieces of a story together in order to create a viable dramatic whole. Approach the structuring of a story in a way that feels comfortable for you. Attainment of this goal doesn't happen overnight. Creating one single story often requires experimenting and planning and falling on your literary rear more than once before you find the way that works for your particular tale. The most important issue is to keep on trying until you get it right.

Eight Approaches to Structuring Your Story

1) *Keep It Simple.* The most fundamental way to look at story is to think of your book as a narrative with a beginning, middle and end. Formulate what each of these means to the plot and how they relate to each other. Then write your story.

- In the beginning, define what your hero wants and why he wants it.

- In the middle, create obstacles the hero must overcome in order to accomplish his goal.

- In the end, resolve the situation in a believable and logical way.

Once you've settled on these fundamentals in your own mind, you can build a story around them, expanding each section and enlarging each plot point.

Beginning, middle and end: the mind, heart and soul of story.

2) *Play It As It Lays.* Make a few notes about your characters and scenes. Get a firm concept in your head of what your book is about. Take a deep breath and begin.

Here, you are winging it, allowing one situation to lead to the next that leads to the next. There's not much advance planning, but there is room for spontaneity.

For most authors, even seasoned ones, this is a risky way to write a book. This open-ended approach makes it too easy to stray from a well-plotted story path. That said, there's no question this method works for some people. Playing it as it lays is analogous to walking down a dark and unfamiliar tunnel using only a tiny flashlight. You can't see very far in front of you, but if you focus carefully on the business at hand, it's possible to make it all the way to the end of the journey without stumbling.

With this approach, you begin by setting your hero in the opening situation and presenting the opening complication. Then you let your characters do the talking and your imagination do the walking.

• *"Watch"* what your characters do, staying open to the latent meaning of their actions.

• *"Listen"* to what your characters have to say, taking advantage of the implications of their dialogue on the page and their whispers in your ear.

When you approach a story in this evolutionary fashion, your ability to access your unconscious and to honor your imagination plays a major role in the creative process.

3) Take Baby Steps. If dealing with the challenges of plot daunts you, break your story into manageable segments that remove the intimidation from the task. Establish the primary story elements of beginning, middle and end. Then envision your narrative as an ongoing, interconnected chain of scene and sequel. One action causes a reaction that causes another action and reaction. Step by step, scene by sequel, you construct one sequence after another, shaping a story—from simple to complex—with these basic building blocks of plot.

For instance, you open with a scene. Then you ask yourself the following questions.

• What is the logical sequel to this scene?

• What action does this scene trigger that leads to the next scene?

• How have I planted the hook to pull the reader into the next scene?

• What has my hero done to move the story along?

• What is the next logical step in the story?

• How does this scene contribute to the larger context of the book?

Using this step-by-step method, you move through your story from the beginning through the middle to the end.

4) Create a Literary Outline. Many of us were taught how to outline written assignments in school, starting with Roman numerals, then moving on to A. B. C., 1. 2. 3., a. b. c. and so forth. You can break down the plot of a book in the same way. Once you've blocked out the story, you can follow the clearly marked trail you've set for yourself from one chapter to the next, from beginning to end.

I hasten to add, however, that while you should think of your outline as an organic whole, you should not think of it as a fixed entity. Don't be afraid to make changes when necessary or to explore a new possibility when characters lead you down a different path.

Before you write your book, break down each chapter into outline form, noting which characters and situations are involved in each chapter. The outline will provide a map to follow and give you an overview of the book. Remember, however, that some of the most interesting journeys involve detours and unexpected sights. So even as you follow the map, stay open to the possibility of surprise.

5) *Walk the North Forty.* Develop a detailed chapter-by-chapter breakdown of your book, creating a visual map to follow. Once you get a grasp on the overview, you can get a better picture of what is happening in your story. When you see those places where you've dropped a plot stitch or where one character hasn't appeared in a while, you can pick up the thread before you move on.

In my first novel, I started writing without a plan. But it soon became evident that I needed a structural guide for my loosely conceived story. With the help of my friend Terry Baker, I eventually created a running chart of my book on shelf paper. A lengthy visual aid, to say the least. I divided the paper into chapter sections with a vertical line. I did the same thing for characters, plot and subplots in horizontal lines that ran through the chapters. Then I wrote down the recurring appearances of various characters in different colored inks. One character was blue. One was red. Another was green. I did the same thing for the plotlines, making notes here and there as reminders that I shouldn't forget to include these things in the book.

When I finally rolled out the diagram across my living room floor and took a look, my entire novel was laid out before me in 12 feet of living color. (Yep, that's right—12 feet!)

To get a sense of what was happening in the book, I strolled the length of my outline like a rancher checking the fence on his north forty. I looked for plot and character omissions. I examined my overlaps and excesses, most of which were immediately apparent after inspecting the chart. If there were no red or green or blue notations for two chapters, I could see that I had to remind the reader about this character or pick up the thread of that subplot. If the plot was dominated by one color, I re-examined the balance I created between characters.

Rather than a four hundred-page novel, I could just as easily apply this system to *The World's Greatest Toe Show*—my sixty-four-page chapter book.

As you can see from the chart on pages 32-33, this strategy can apply to both fiction and nonfiction, short books and long ones. I have used variations on this approach for several of my more complicated children's novels. And each time I do it I gain comfort and confidence from the concrete visualization the chart provides.

6) Decorate Your Wall. Make scene-by-scene notes on 3"x5" cards and arrange them on a bulletin board. The advantage of this method is that you can move your cards around, add some and toss others, without messing up your overall story.

If a bulletin board is too confining, choose a door or a blank wall. Then use Post-it Notes to define characters and create scenes. Not only do these notes now come in different colors, they also come in different sizes.

Color coding characters and plot themes is helpful when you use these methods because you can see what character or theme or plot point is missing.

7) Go Classical. Honor the old ways and follow classical story structure of Greek drama from the exciting force to the climax to the resolution. I'll cover this method in detail in chapters five and nine.

8) Mix and Match. Do your own thing. Consider all the different ways to structure your story and choose the methods you prefer. If you want to mix scene and sequel with a literary map, do it. Find the combination that's right for you.

Keep in mind that none of these approaches are carved in stone. There are lots of options, and you are not obligated to follow any of them. As I said before, the best way to structure your story is to do what works

CHARTING YOUR BOOK BY CHAPTERS

	Action	Main Characters Emily, Spike, Tulu, Billy, Frankie
Chapter 1	Discuss fair Emily's revelation	Talk about the school fair
Chapter 2	See toe Plan toe show	Look at toe Make plans
Chapter 3	School: Curiosity Home: Planning	Preparation for the fair
Chapter 4	Fair Decorate booth	Keep parents and teachers away from booth
Chapter 5	Fair Shock and horror	Kids show off toe
Chapter 6	Fair Chaos Award	Teachers and principal confront kids And the winners are: The Canal Street Gang ties with Bunny and Violetta
Chapter 7	Club meeting Toe disposal Serious discussion	Discuss what should be done with the toe
Chapter 8	Funeral for the toe	Eulogy for the toe Cremation of the toe

CHARTING YOUR BOOK BY CHAPTERS

	POV Characters Emily	Subplot Bunny and Violetta
Chapter 1	Emily's revelation	Canal Street Gang discuss rivalry, but Bunny and Violetta aren't seen
Chapter 2	Emily shows toe	Bunny and Violetta mentioned by Canal Street Gang
Chapter 3	Emily meets Bunny and Violetta	
Chapter 4	Emily avoids teacher's questions about toe	Bunny and Violetta make fun of Canal Street booth Bunny and Violetta are curious about the toe show
Chapter 5	Emily lures Bunny into booth	Bunny sees toe and is horrified She screams, spills the toe on the ground Chaos!
Chapter 6	Emily confesses to her father that she has his toe	Teachers and Mr. Anderson confront Canal Street Gang Bunny and Violetta are left sulking
Chapter 7	Emily meets with gang to discuss what will happen to toe	
Chapter 8	Emily hides ashes of the toe to save for next school fair	

for you. Whatever method you choose, however, the most important thing to remember is to trust in your story, honor the fundamental conventions of plot and structure, and promise yourself to finish what you set out to do.

Your Turn
Design Your Own Structure

OK, now you try it. Take the story you're working on and ask yourself the following question: Am I a fly-by-the-seat-of-my-pants kind of person or a take-control-and-eliminate-surprises kind of person?

If you're a fly-by-the-seat-of-my-pants person, organize your book according to the suggestions in numbers one through three on pages 28–29.

If you're a take-control person, organize your book using the suggestions in numbers four through seven on pages 29–31.

If more than one approach appeals to you, try number eight on page 31.

This is the time to experiment with different methods. If one doesn't seem like a good fit, try another. As you work, ask yourself the following questions.

- Which method gives me the most confidence in writing my story?
- Which method makes me feel the most comfortable?
- Which method allows me to move from beginning to end with the most ease?
- Which method offers me the greatest chance of finishing my book?

Don't be afraid to commit to a method and start writing your book. But if you get stuck, don't be afraid to make a change. This is the time to try out several different ways to structure your story until you find one that suits your temperament, gives you courage and fuels your creativity.

CHAPTER FIVE

Breaking Ground: How to Begin the Beginning

My way is to begin at the beginning.

—*Lord Byron,* Don Juan

ONE, TWO, THREE—GO!

A practical fact: If you don't capture an editor's interest at the beginning of a book, it's unlikely you will have that editor's attention for the rest of the book. At the most, you've got two or three pages to hook the reader. That is a writer's reality, especially a first-time writer's reality. With rare exceptions, if you don't accomplish story-telling magic immediately, your manuscript will be tossed onto the publisher's paper mountain commonly referred to as—*dum-de-dum-dum*—The Rejection Pile. Then, if you've included a self-addressed stamped envelope, your manuscript will eventually be returned along with a polite form letter from the editor saying the story that you've slaved over for the past eight months isn't right for their list or doesn't fit the publisher's needs at this time.

It won't matter that pages 10 to 160 of your middle-grade novel are some of the most awesome and compelling ever written in the annals of children's literature. Chances are those pages won't be read as long as they are preceded by a weak beginning.

I doubt if today's young readers are going to give you the three-page grace period that editors might. Television and the Internet have shortened the attention spans of most kids. What worked in books fifty years ago doesn't necessarily work now. There are notable exceptions, of course. J.K. Rowling's Harry Potter books prove that with the right combination of enthusiastic peers, intriguing characters, exciting suspense, thematic connections and interesting plots, children are happy to read long and involved stories. This does not change the fact, however, that if you don't hook the reader on the first page, you run the risk of his moving on to another book.

An intriguing beginning anchors the story. It gives the writer a strong sense of the narrative and the reader a powerful need to know what happens next.

THE GIFT OF THE GREEKS

In classical drama, the Greeks called the opening scene the exciting force. This is the dramatic incident that triggers the rising motion—the initial complication of the plot—and imbues your story with the necessary velocity to carry it from the beginning through the middle to the end.

The exciting force is the catalyst for your entire story and sets up the conflict of opposing interests: This is what your hero wants, and this is why he can't have it. If the exciting force is not strong enough or powerful enough, your plot won't have the necessary forward momentum to sustain the reader's interest.

Imagine that your story is a spaceship preparing to take off for a journey to the moon. This particular trip has three distinct parts analogous to the beginning, middle and end: the movement through the Earth's atmosphere, the travel across open space and the landing on the Moon.

Your spaceship—your story—cannot travel out of the Earth's atmosphere to its final destination if the booster rockets are not powerful enough to thrust it beyond the planet's gravitational pull. In fact, if your booster rockets fail, your spaceship will fall back to Earth and burn into embers.

Think of your opening, your exciting force, as your booster rockets. Then construct your story accordingly, keeping in mind the following six essentials when you create your opening paragraphs. You can use one or two of these techniques, or you can use all of them. The choice is up to you.

Six Considerations for the Opening Gambit

1) Give the Reader a Sense of What the Book Is About. In the beginning, the author presents a contract to readers, letting them know what kind of book they are going to read.

In *The Great Mosquito, Bull and Coffin Caper,* a middle-grade novel I wrote, the opening paragraph reads:

> There are lots of things I hate in this world. I hate peas and squash and multiplication tables. I hate going to bed before I'm sleepy. I hate having a stupid older brother, too. But most of all, more than anything else in the world, I hate losing my best friend.

What information is conveyed in that opening paragraph? How do you know what the book is about?

We know this character has a distinct voice. We know this kid has problems with his older brother. We know this is a kid who's not only angry about something, he's given to exaggeration. We also know that this is a kid who's about to lose his best friend.

Those are all absorbing story elements to an eight-year-old reader—elements designed to draw her into the book on the first page.

2) Uncover a Problem. Some books state the problem right away. Others just hint at it. Either way, the reader can get a good sense of what the conflict might be.

At the picture book level, Maurice Sendak accomplishes this goal in *Where the Wild Things Are.*

> The night Max wore his wolf suit and made mischief of one kind and another . . . he was sent to bed without eating anything.

The problem here is that a boy is making mischief and talking back to his mother. We know he's going to pay a price for this behavior. We're not sure yet what that price will be, but we do know the story will continue beyond the immediate consequence of getting sent to bed without his supper. The reader naturally wants to discover what's going to happen next.

3) Reveal Character. Sometimes revelation is accomplished in a subtle way with the author hinting at the kind of kid the hero is. Other times the emotional state of the protagonist is apparent from the opening sentence.

In J.D. Salinger's *The Catcher in the Rye*, Holden Caulfield, the adolescent hero, begins his story with:

> If you really want to hear about it, the first thing you'll probably want to know is where I was born, and what my lousy childhood was like, and how my parents were occupied and all before they had me, and all that David Copperfield kind of crap, but I don't feel like going into it, if you want to know the truth.

This is a kid with a powerful voice. He's tough and resentful and thinks he's smart enough to know what the reader really wants. He's also filled with a sad and naked anger. This is a hero who's railing against the world—a hero teenagers can relate to.

Because of its voice and its perfect-pitch portrait of a disaffected American teen, *The Catcher in the Rye* is as relevant today as it was when it was first published more than fifty years ago.

4) Pose a Question to the Reader. When written skillfully, creating implicit questions is a technique guaranteed to hook a reader.

In *Ellen Foster*, a crossover novel for teens and adults, Kaye Gibbons opens her story with:

> When I was little I would think of ways to kill my daddy. I would figure out this or that way and run it down through my head until it got easy.
> The way I liked best was letting go a poisonous spider in his bed.

What questions are posed here? The first question that springs to mind is, why does this girl want to kill her father? What has he done—what

was horrible enough—to make her want to kill him? Does the girl succeed in killing her father? These questions create a powerful engine that
drives the book and immediately hooks the reader.

In just two sentences, Conrad Richter manages to pose a quiet but
irresistible question in his YA novel *The Light in the Forest.*

> The boy was about fifteen years old. He tried to stand very
> straight and still when he heard the news, but inside of
> him everything had gone black.

Why was the boy trying to stand tall? What had happened to force him
to make this effort? What was the news that was dreadful enough to
cause everything inside him to go black?

5) Hint at the Conflict to Come. Conflict is the engine that drives story.
Conflict can be comical or dramatic, scary or tragic. If a character doesn't
confront and cope with conflict, she can't grow or change. And without
this transformation, the character isn't interesting to read about.

K.A. Applegate's opening to *Animorphs: The Invasion* is as riveting as
it is mysterious. It also contains portents of the conflict to come.

> My name is Jake. That's my first name, obviously. I can't
> tell you my last name. It would be too dangerous. The Con-
> trollers are everywhere.

Why is this boy in danger? Why can't he tell you his last name? What
kind of danger is he in? And who are the Controllers? All of these urgent
and powerful questions are posed in just twenty-five words. The hint of
future conflict is contained in the questions. We know the Controllers
are after the boy. And we suspect the boy will have to confront the
Controllers—sooner, rather than later. That's what makes us want to
continue reading.

6) Anchor the Story in Time and Space. From the beginning, readers
not only like to know what the story is about, they like to know where
it takes place and in what period of time in history.

In *Jenny of the Tetons*, by Kristiana Gregory, the book informs the reader immediately about time and space.

> Our wagon train, what was left of it, pulled into Fort Hall just after sundown. July heat smothered the darkening desert. A cluster of tipis around the outer walls only increased my terror.

This paragraph informs the reader that the story takes place in nineteenth-century America in the desert. The reader knows immediately what kind of story is going to be told. This information is particularly helpful to those readers who have distinct preferences about the books they read. Marianne doesn't like science fiction, Ricardo doesn't like animal stories and Joann doesn't like thrillers. These kinds of readers especially appreciate knowing early on what kind of book they have picked up.

◦◦◦

For all-time outrageous comical originality in the opening of a novel, my nomination goes to Daniel Pinkwater's *Young Adult Novel*. This one poses questions, uncovers problems, reveals character and hints at conflict. And if a reader is already familiar with Pinkwater's fractured sensibility, it will probably make him laugh.

This book has an opening that imprints itself indelibly on a kid's imagination and makes him want to continue reading beyond the first page.

> Kevin's new social worker was Mr. Justin Jarvis, and Kevin didn't like him one bit. He was constantly smiling, and he spoke in a smooth, soft voice that made Kevin nervous.
> Most annoying was the knowledge that Kevin depended on Mr. Jarvis completely. Kevin's mother was in the madhouse. . . . She had gone mad the day Kevin's father had been in the accident at the methane works—the day he had been deprived of speech, sight, and hearing, and the use of his legs. Dad was in the veteran's hospital now, little better than a vegetable.

OK, OK. I know this opening is far out. Actually, Kevin's story is purely fiction, a story within a story. But for the right kid with the right—i.e., twisted—sense of humor, the opening is also utterly inspired.

BEGINNING THE BEGINNING

Now that you've examined the various ways to hook a reader at the beginning of a book, consider the story you are working on. Ask yourself how you can apply these techniques to your own book. Which approaches create a strong fit with the tale you want to tell? Make a serious effort to figure out ways to apply some of these ideas to your opening pages as you read the setups the following authors have used.

Your Turn
Opening Exercises

1) *Their beginnings.* Consider the openings from the following books and analyze why they work.

From *Charlotte's Web* by E.B. White (middle-grade novel)

"Where's Papa going with that ax?" said Fern to her mother as they were setting the table for breakfast.
"Out to the hoghouse," replied Mrs. Arable. "Some pigs were born last night."

From *Tower of Evil* by Mary Main (YA novel)

Fog gives me the creeps. I'm not talking about the cool mist that burns off the ocean on summer mornings. That's romantic, poetic, even. I mean the heavy gray stuff that seeps through your pores into your skin until you can't stop shivering. That's the kind of fog that wrapped itself around me as I hiked over the dunes on my first day in California.

From *Hey, Kid!* by Rita Golden Gelman (early reader)

"Hey, Kid!"
"Who me?"
"I have this thing.
It's white and black and gray.
I'm gonna let you have it, Kid.
Today's your lucky day."

From *Harry Potter and the Sorcerer's Stone* by J.K. Rowling (middle-grader and up)

Mr. and Mrs. Dursley, of number four, Privet Drive, were proud to say that they were perfectly normal, thank you very much. They were the last people you'd expect to be involved in anything strange or mysterious, because they just didn't hold with such nonsense.

2) *Your beginning.* Now that you've read the openings of other books and thought about why they work, it's time to create your own beginning. Write two opening paragraphs for a book about a boy or girl meeting someone important.
Include the following elements.

• Introduce a memorable character.

• Create or hint at the problem or conflict the hero must face.

• Offer the reason why this problem is hard to solve.

• State, or at least imply, what the boy or girl intends to do about it.

• Anchor the beginning in time and space.

• Write these paragraphs in the most economical fashion possible.

Don't be afraid to experiment. The heroine doesn't need to be meeting her father. She can be meeting anyone anywhere for any purpose—a friend at Victoria Station in London, a sister on a ranch in Pecos, New

Mexico, or a mysterious stranger at a restaurant in Seattle, Washington. As an example of one way to approach this exercise and include all these elements, check out step 3 below. Then, take a deep breath, give your imagination full rein, and let it run.

3) *My sample beginning.* Here's my entry into the opening sweepstakes. Keep in mind that this is merely *one* example of *one* way to open a story. There are as many ways to approach this subject as there are writers to write about it.

As Jake waited on the platform of the train station, he wondered what the man would look like. They'd never met. All Jake knew was that his father had called him on his birthday and said he had something important to give him. Not that Jake gave a damn. He'd lived this long without a father and saw no reason to change that now.

In the distance, the train whistled long and low. What once was familiar and comforting turned into a sad and lonely sound. Jake was tempted to leave. Just walk away from the one-room North Dakota train station and disappear into the searing August day. He doubted his father would care. The man had been given twelve years to do that. And Jake had never heard a word from him until now.

CHAPTER SIX

The Beginning, Continued

The difference between truth and fiction is that fiction has to make sense.

—*Mark Twain*

WHAT NOW?

Now comes the hard part. You've written this hot opening paragraph or two, but you wonder what to do next. Somehow you've got to propel the action forward by moving the exciting force onto center stage. You've got to catch the reader and pull her into the story. You've got to hold her hand so tight, entangle her so skillfully in the lives of the characters that she won't want to let go.

How do you accomplish this goal? You analyze your opening and tell the story that evolves out of it.

THREE APPROACHES TO STORYTELLING

There are three basic ways to handle the rest of this particular story: the Forward March, the Total Flashback, or the Zig-Zag Method. As you might guess, however, there is wiggle room within each of these conventions that allows you to create your own variations on these basic themes.

THE FORWARD MARCH

The first way to approach the continuation of the story is to move forward in time in a linear fashion. You go from A to B to C to D to E. No stopping, no doubling back. The plot moves in strict chronological order.

Advantages of the Forward March

• It's a simple technique to master.

• Moving the story ahead in a linear fashion avoids literary traps and convoluted plot devices.

• It's easy to organize a plot in this way.

Disadvantages of the Forward March

• It's hard to tell a complete and textured story without shifting back and forth in time.

• Without the use of flashbacks, your storytelling options are limited.

At the beginning of my writing career, I wrote for adults. But when I shifted to writing for children, I took the lessons I had learned and applied them to children's books.

When I wrote my first novel, I had never taken a writing class. As a consequence, I wasn't consciously aware of techniques authors use to create a story. All I knew was that I was an enthusiastic reader, a good writer, and I had a story I wanted to tell. The problem was, I didn't know how to go about telling it.

One of the first challenges I encountered was how to move from one point in time to another. After writing the first ten pages of the book, I came to a screeching halt when I realized I didn't know how to make a transition in time or space. The practical consequence of this lack of basic knowledge was that I couldn't move from one scene to the next.

A writer friend of mine named David Markson suggested I solve the challenge of structuring the plot by writing the book in strict chronological order. Grateful for his encouragement of my naive efforts, I took his suggestion. As a matter of fact, I applied a literal interpretation to his advice, allotting one chapter for each day of the week. The novel began on a Sunday and finished on a Saturday. Each chapter opened in the morning and closed at night. No skipping, no doubling back. Structure 101.

With that concept in mind, let's return to Jake at the train station and see how this story might play out in a straightforward, chronological way.

> . . . In the distance, the train whistled long and low. What once was familiar and comforting turned into a sad and lonely sound. Jake was tempted to leave. Just walk away from the one-room North Dakota train station and disappear into the hot August day. He doubted his father would care. The man had been given twelve years to do that. And Jake had never heard a word from him until now.
>
> Jake stood silent, barely able to see. He wished he hadn't asked his mom to stay home. He'd never felt more alone in his life. As the train rounded the brown dusty hill in the distance and bore down on the station, Jake's heart beat faster and his breathing took on the rhythm of the engine. Chuga chuga, chuga chuga.
>
> He held his back straight, his hands at his side. The knuckles turned white on his clenched fists.
>
> Chuga . . . Chuga . . . Chuga . . . Sssssssssssss.
>
> Jake's breath caught in his throat as the train pulled to a stop. Oh God, he thought, please don't let him hate me. His stomach twisted into an impossible knot as a man—dark, brush-cut hair, black eyes and a nervous expression on his face—stepped onto the platform and looked around. He carried a small suitcase and a package the size of a shoe box wrapped in brown paper.
>
> "Jake?" he said.
>
> Jake nodded. Then he stepped forward to meet the stranger who was his father.

If this were a short, middle-grade novel, we could end the first section here, either with a chapter break or a double-space. We leave the scene with plenty of unanswered questions. We have also created the need to know what happens next and what's in the package.

In the next section, we could pick up on the father and son walking away from the station. The story is told in linear fashion—a straight journey forward into the future as one scene unfolds into the next. From the initial meeting at the train station, we move through Jake's first awkward moments with his dad. Then the boy and the man walk to the two-story hotel where the dad checks in before he takes Jake to lunch. He doesn't let the mysterious package leave his side.

We continue through the story as Jake tries to resist falling under the spell of his charismatic father. Maybe his mom and dad could get back together again, he thinks. At the same time he's entertaining this possibility, Jake struggles with the push-pull feelings directed at a father who abandoned him before he was born.

As the story unfolds, we watch as Jake gradually comes to understand that his wish for his parents' reconciliation is doomed to failure. And in the process, we witness how painful the eventual meeting is for his mother.

In this straightforward approach to telling this tale, we move in chronological order through the story, from A to Z without any flashbacks, without any movement back and forth in time. The momentum is always toward the future, never the past.

THE FLASHBACK

A flashback is used when you want to shift from the present action of the story into the past. There are several reasons you might want to do this.

- To clue the reader in on a secret about the hero's earlier life

- To give some background information about a specific plot element

- To give the reader some background information about the subplot

- To contribute to the development of a subplot

- To enlighten the reader about a particular aspect of a character

- To add texture and complexity to a character

There are two basic ways to approach the flashback. Each one occupies an important place in storytelling.

The Total Flashback

Using this technique, you would tell the story of Jake standing at the train station in an entirely different way than if you just move forward in time. For instance, you could open the story with the section that takes place in the present. Then you would shift back to an earlier point in time. In the Total Flashback, you stay in the past, telling the back story of the hero until you work your way up to the present again—the moment when Jake meets his father.

If you take this approach, the first section can even be written as a prologue. You move from present to past to present. Full circle.

Advantages of the Total Flashback.
- It opens up the story to the past and allows you to include all sorts of information that would be absent in the strict chronological telling of a tale.
- You can add critical back stories that lend texture and depth to your narrative.
- You can convey information about the character and his life that otherwise might be lost.
- With the exception of the initial flashback, you still have the simplicity of dealing with a fundamentally forward-moving plot.

Disadvantages of the Total Flashback.
- It's a more demanding technique to master.
- Unless this approach is executed with skill, the young reader could get confused about what's happening in the past and what's happening in the present.

In the Total Flashback method, we carry the story to the point where the father steps off the train. Then we move back in time and live through Jake's attempts to find his father, watching as he encounters one obstacle after another.

> . . . Jake's breath caught in his throat as the train pulled to a stop. Oh God, he thought, please don't let me hate him. Don't let me hate my father. And don't let him bring me something awful that I'm stuck with for the rest of my life.

The boy stood paralyzed, trying to fathom why he had chosen to meet this man. He and his mom had a good life. They loved each other and got along just fine without a husband and father.

All things considered, Jake's life was fine the way it was. He had good friends and a dog named Duke—a black mutt with a tan snout and eyebrows, and a white stripe on his nose. The boy and dog went everywhere together, except school and church.

Jake's mom gave him the puppy around the time he started asking questions about his father. He was six years old, getting ready to begin first grade.

"Why don't I have a dad?" Jake had asked at the dinner table one night. Grandpa cleared his throat and looked down at his plate. His grandma picked up a platter and carried it to the kitchen.

"Why, Mom?"

Susan Davidson reached across the table and took her son's hand. A soft sigh escaped her lips.

"Scott has a dad and so does Mike," said Jake. "Even though Tilly's parents are divorced, she's got a dad. He writes to her and calls her. And every summer and every Christmas she goes to live with him in Bismarck."

"Your dad left before you were born," Jake's mom said. Her voice was quiet, showing little emotion. "I don't know where he is."

"What's his name?"

"Nathan. Nathan Sinclair."

"Someday I'm going to meet that man and ask him why he left me," Jake said.

You've got the idea. I've shifted the story back in time to when Jake was six years old. We then follow his life as he begins the search for his father, the one thing he wants to find more than anything in the world.

In this approach, we witness how each lead he follows momentarily raises his hopes before it turns into another dead end. Then, for his eleventh birthday, Jake gets a computer. Three months later, in exchange for his promise to gather the eggs every morning and take them by Chow's grocery on the way to school, his grandpa signs him on to the Internet.

That's when the search for the father begins in earnest.

As you can see, we've set up the reader with certain expectations for the character. And it is our obligation to meet every one of them. When you use the flashback technique, you make implicit promises to—and contracts with—your reader. The following techniques can help you do this.

The Fundamentals of the Total Flashback

Play Catch-Up. Even though you've gone back in time, the reader naturally assumes you will move forward until you finally arrive at the train station again. This is the contract you set up when you move into a flashback. And it is a contract you must not break.

Dramatize Critical Scenes. Another aspect of your contract with the reader is that you will play out the meeting with the father in full. That is the promise you made in the opening paragraphs. You cannot have Jake meet his dad "offstage," so to speak, referring to the meeting without ever dramatizing it in present time. Nor can you have Jake meet his dad on the last page of the story and leave the reader hanging, O. Henry style. That's dirty pool—especially for young readers—even though you might have gone to all sorts of trouble to set up endless reasons for not playing out the story any further.

Calculate Timing. In carrying out the terms of your contract, you should have Jake and his father come together at the station about two-thirds to three-quarters of the way through the book. This gives you ample opportunity to play out the story in present time, to find out what's in the package, and to wrap up the plot about Jake and his father. You also have time to play out the subplots of his mother's fear of losing her son to this interloper and the mending of her strained relationship with the man she once loved.

Create a Powerful Opening Scene. In the Total Flashback, it is critical that you set up an opening scene powerful and memorable enough for the reader to want to return to it. This provides a strong anchor for the reader, one that keeps the story line steady and marks the point of return.

If you just have Jake going to the train station and waiting for someone, that wouldn't make the reader want to stick around long enough to find out who he's meeting or what he's doing there. You need to pose questions the reader wants answered. Questions powerful enough for her to stick around in order to have her curiosity satisfied.

• Why hasn't Jake ever met his father?

• What happened between Jake's mom and dad?

• Why hasn't the father even bothered to send his son a card?

• What if Jake and his dad don't get along?

• Why has the father contacted his son after all these years?

• What is this special thing the father wants to give his son?

Anchor the Story. When dealing with a flashback, it's important to be clear about when the flashback takes place in relation to the opening scene. This kind of clarity anchors the story in the reader's mind and avoids the confusion that so many flashbacks create.

What have we learned in the opening paragraphs that anchors the scene in the reader's mind?

• Jake is twelve years old when he goes to the train station. He's alone, and he's scared as he waits to meet this stranger who happens to be his father.

• The connection is made between his new puppy and his first questions about his father as we flash back to when Jake was six years old. This informs the reader that there is a six-year period of time that must be spanned in order to return to the present, creating both an anchor and a time frame to orient the reader, informing her where she has come from and where she is going.

These are elements that not only intrigue the reader but create expectations. Just as keeping a promise is not optional, the observation of the rituals that inform the reader and resolve the story are not optional, either. If you keep all your promises to the reader, the reader will honor you by sticking with your story until the end.

THE ZIG-ZAG METHOD

The flashback has a long and venerable history as a story-telling device. You can use it in one grand, full-circle sweep, as in the Total Flashback method above. Or you can write the story in a forward timeline until you reach a moment where you need to fill in some detail from the past or add a particularly suspenseful or memorable scene. Then you slip into a mini-flashback before returning to the present-time story.

Advantages of the Zig-Zag Method.
• The technique allows you to provide needed background material whenever you want to include it.

• You can use this technique to pique the curiosity of the reader.

• You can use the Zig-Zag in order to increase suspense.

• You can work in critical information as you move forward with the plot.

Disadvantages of the Zig-Zag Method.
• It's a more challenging technique to master.

• Unless this approach is used with skill, the reader can get confused between past and present story lines.

The Zig-Zag Method is a common and stimulating way to tell a story, but it can be confusing if it's used awkwardly. Here, you combine both of the previous approaches, except the action does not move back in time and stay there for long stretches. Instead, you provide the missing pieces in the form of quick strokes as you go along.

Let's return to the railroad station one more time and play the scene this way.

> . . . Jake stood silent, barely able to see the train tracks. He wished he hadn't asked his mom to stay home. Ever since he was a little boy he'd depended on her presence to make him feel safe. Jake knew he could always count on his mom's help. Even when he was teased about not having a father and he beat the living daylights out of Eddie Sanchez, his mom was there for him.
>
> Now, on this hot August day, Jake had never felt more alone

in his life. As the train rounded the brown, dusty hill in the distance and bore down on the station, his heart beat faster and his breathing took on the rhythm of the engine. Chuga chuga, chuga chuga.

He held his back straight, his hands at his side. The knuckles turned white on his clenched fists.

Chuga . . . Chuga . . . Chuga . . . Sssssssssss.

Jake stood paralyzed as the train pulled to a stop. For the life of him, he couldn't figure out why he had decided to meet this man—this stranger.

I must be crazy, he thought. Mom and I have a good life. We get along . . . most of the time, anyway. Why did I ever decide to mess with it? His mom certainly hadn't been pleased.

"Are you sure you know what you are doing?" she had asked when Jake told her he had contacted his father. They had been gathering eggs when he broke the news.

"Of course I know," Jake had said.

"I hope you're right," his mom had said. Her voice shook as she lay a speckled brown egg in the basket she carried.

Once Jake thought about his decision, he wasn't so sure he had done the right thing. He wondered if the letter he wrote to his father would change his life forever. He wasn't so sure he could deal with that. Or that he wanted to.

Jake liked living on the farm. He was close enough to town to see his friends and far enough away to have the freedom of the wide-open spaces. For as long as he could remember, Jake had had his own horse. First it was just an old nag. Then, for his tenth birthday, his grandpa had given him a sorrel quarter horse named Socks.

Jake also had a dog named Duke. The boy and dog went everywhere together, except school and church. It was hard to leave Duke home on this particular day. But Jake didn't want anything to distract him from his mission. Besides, Duke was scared of trains.

Jake watched the engine as it pulled to a stop at the station.

Or what passed as a station in Shiloh, North Dakota, population 927.

His breath caught in his throat. Oh God, he thought, please don't let me hate him. His stomach twisted into an impossible knot as a man stepped onto the platform and looked around.

"Jake?" he said.

Jake nodded and stepped forward to meet the stranger who was his father.

As you can see, this method is something of a dance—a minuet in which you touch and then you let go. You move back to color in a spot of background, and you move forward to continue the story. One step forward, one step back; five steps forward, two steps back. If this is done skillfully, the reader isn't even aware of the changes in time. You're simply filling in details as you come to them.

Occasionally, you might include a longer flashback. But you always return to a strong scene in the present.

Your Turn
Choosing the Way

One story, three ways to tell it. I've shown you how to do it. Now it's your turn.

1) Take that opening you wrote, the one about the meeting with a stranger. Then write it again, experimenting with the three different ways to tell your story.

- The Forward March

- The Total Flashback

- The Zig-Zag Method

Write five pages for each approach—enough so you get a firm feel for the story and how you're going to deal with the challenges your beginning presents.

Remember: You are focusing on *storytelling*. Use the techniques you've learned to draw the reader into your story by making him want to know what happens next.

2) Once you've written your pages, go back over each technique and ask yourself the following questions.

- Did I present my contract clearly?
- Did I pose interesting questions?
- Have I created a compelling conflict?
- Have I uncovered an interesting problem?
- Have I presented an interesting character?
- Have I given the reader a hero to root for?
- Have I built an intriguing foundation?
- Above all, have I kept all my promises?

Return to the beginning of each version, and revise it until all these questions are answered in the affirmative.

3) Now it's time to decide which way you want to tell your story. At this point, you can ask yourself the following questions.

- Which technique makes me feel the most comfortable?
- Which story stands out from the other two?
- Which technique is the best fit for the story I want to tell?
- What is the strongest way to tell the story?

Once you've answered these questions and settled on an approach you want to use, it's time to continue.

CHAPTER SEVEN

The Spoiler Wars

It's easy, after all, not to be a writer.
Most people aren't writers, and very little harm comes to them.

—Julian Barnes

YOUR MOVE

Here's the situation: You've just written a terrific opening. You've created a razzle-dazzle, whoop-de-doo, bang-up beginning to your story. You have accomplished all the goals you set for yourself. You've hinted at conflict, posed interesting questions, presented a problem, created great characters and hooked the reader. You've done everything right. At this point you might be tempted to ask, "Where do I go from here? How do I peel this fabulous fictional onion I just had the temerity to create?"

Trust me on this point: If you are anxious about what to do next, you're not alone. There are few writers who have moved past the opening of their books without wondering how to proceed.

The answer to this dilemma is simple and straightforward: What you do next grows out of what you've already done. One thing leads to another that leads to another. To borrow from Robert Frost, you've got promises to keep.

THE INHERENT SENSE OF STORY

Unlike in life, in storytelling things happen for a reason. In fiction, every event demands a cause. And every cause demands an effect. If you plant a seed, it must sprout. Furthermore, you must plant the seed in front of the reader before you show her the sprout. These are the rules. I hasten to add that Dickens and his ilk who traffic successfully in coincidence and surprise are rare exceptions to those rules. But we mere storytelling mortals are doomed to follow them. Otherwise, we lose our credibility with our readers.

Following the rules is one thing. Making sense of the random nature of the universe is another. To feel overwhelmed is a natural response to the multiple challenges of storytelling. You've just tossed these introductory balls in the air; now, how do you keep them there? How do you juggle all those plot points without dropping one or two or all of them?

Chaos Theory may apply to the universe of subatomic particles. But it does not apply to the universe of fiction. Just as quantum physicists posit that the fundamental unity of life can be found in Superstring Theory, writers must create a fundamental unity of story in their own fictional world. In fact, it is the writer's singular task to gather together the disparate elements of plot and character and integrate them into a cohesive whole. Boiled down to its essence, storytelling is no more than the imposition of order on imagined experience.

Making sense of the events in your story so they make sense to your reader is a critical goal of fiction. To my mind, the only time you can get away with a genuine, random event is at the opening of the book. Something happens. Something unanticipated. Something unusual. Something fabulous or puzzling or horrific. This event—the exciting force—then sets off a chain reaction. These actions and reactions comprise the middle of your story and lead to the inevitable end.

Whether you tell this story in flashback, mini-flashbacks or in chronological order, the rest of your book grows out of those opening events.

ENTER THE SPOILER

About the time you reach the beginning of the middle of your book, your most destructive internal critic steps out of the wings and onto the stage of your consciousness. With her mouth pursed and her arms crossed, a nasty smile flickers across her lips. She's been waiting for this moment.

"Everyone knows you're a fake," she says with a squint-eyed smirk. "What *ever* made you think you could write a book?" Stunned, you step back. The Spoiler moves in for the kill. "You got yourself into this mess." Significant pause. "*Now* let's see you get out of it!" We've all got Spoilers. Men have them. Women have them. This is not a gender-specific role. My Spoiler happens to be female and speaks in a whisper. But a Spoiler might just as well have a voice that makes pronouncements in a basso profundo and belongs to a man who shaves three times a day. For our purposes, however, the Spoiler will henceforth be referred to as female.

So instead of cowering before this literary ogre, take a deep breath and tell that double-dealing, undermining, life-negating, confidence-stealing petty tyrant to shut her mouth, back off your personal stage and stay in the basement where she belongs.

Truth in Advertising

I've just given you great advice. Remember it. Cherish it. Place it at the front of your creative shelf so you can stroke it every day. In the interest of truth, however, I'm forced to confess that this gem of wisdom—this hard-won, life-polished pearl of perspicacity—falls into that familiar but slippery category labeled "Easier Said Than Done."

The reason your internal voice has gotten away with its negative nonsense for so long is that you haven't paid attention to it, at least consciously. This Darth Vader of the psyche has probably been whispering in your ear all your life. In fact, most of these toxic tapes run on a continuous loop.

You become so used to hearing the venomous voices, you don't even register them with your conscious mind. That doesn't mean, however, your unconscious mind isn't picking up on the content. So your task as a writer—and as a human being—is to become aware of these voices in order to mute their impact and to allow you to live the full creative life you deserve.

I can personally attest to the fact that becoming aware of, as well as transforming, our negative internal messages is one of life's greatest challenges. I have put my shrink's two kids through college in my efforts to quell my own voices that, to date, have proven they know how to manifest defeat in 731 ways.

That said, given that I've had more than a tad of experience in this field of study, I can offer you some hard-won advice.

Thoughts From a Wounded Veteran of the Spoiler Wars

• If you don't face the Spoiler now, she'll taunt you for the rest of your book. Or, more likely, for the rest of your life. And she'll do her best to convince you to give up writing while you can still find regular, reliable, long-term employment that occupies you both day *and* night.

• Confronting the voices is like quitting smoking. There's never a good time to do it. Therefore, the best time to tackle this challenge is now.

• Just because the voices speak to you from within doesn't mean they speak the truth.

• Negative voices run on automatic pilot and depend on you to do the same. That's how they become an integral part of your creative wallpaper and assume so much power.

• The way to mute the intensity of the message is to become aware of the voices and how they undermine your confidence.

As you lie in bed and do your deep-belly breathing, open yourself to the thoughts that drift past you in wispy, barely heard whispers. The ones that say things like:

"Psst! Give up now before you embarrass yourself."

"You never were any good at finishing a task."

"You're not (choose three of the following adjectives and fill in the blanks below: smart/skilled/talented/creative/deserving/clever/wise/imaginative/productive/disciplined/capable/qualified/educated/experienced/gifted/inventive/realistic/interesting) enough to pull this book off."

_____ _____ _____

(fill in the blanks)

• Make an effort to identify the voices. Ask yourself where these voices came from and who they belong to.

Your mother?

Your father?

Your third-grade teacher?

Your old lover?

Your older sibling?

Your grandparent?

Your ex?

Your nanny?

Your internal child?

Identifying the speakers isn't always possible. But if you can put a face to the voice, it helps remove the sting from the words.

• When you hear the voices, learn to identify the feelings that accompany them. Once you've got a handle on what the feelings are, allow yourself to experience them both physically and emotionally, then let them go (this is another one of those Easier-Said-Than-Done situations).

• Every time you hear the voice, acknowledge its presence but not its power. Remind yourself that this is a voice, not a reality. It no longer speaks to you with authority.

Sometimes you'll only catch a phrase or a few well-chosen words.

You're only . . .

You'll never . . .

You can't . . .

I can't believe you did such a stupid . . .

But if you listen carefully as you go about your daily tasks—if you practice awareness—you'll begin to understand that voices are running in the back of your mind all day long. They're accustomed to being able to speak undisturbed. The mere fact that you make the voices conscious is enough to diminish some of their power.

• Once you become aware of the messages, you can begin to replace them with more positive words.

Creativity is a natural part of my being.

This is a terrific idea for a book, and I am the one to write it.

Just because I've never written a book before doesn't mean I can't write one now.

I am wise enough to know what I don't know. I am smart enough to learn what I don't know. And I am talented enough to write what I do know.

Think *The Little Engine That Could.*

Warning!

Identification of the voices is not enough. In order to keep the Spoiler in check, you must make awareness a lifelong habit. This is a reasonable price to pay for creative freedom.

Reality Check

You never get rid of the Spoiler. You can't just spray Raid over the dark corners of your psyche, poison the creepy-crawly negativity and be done with it. But you can make consciousness an integral part of your daily life. In doing this, you take away the power of the voice and expand the parameters and possibilities of your creative life.

Your Turn
Take on the Spoiler

Use this Negative Message Disposal Technique whenever you're assaulted by the Spoiler.

- Make a list of as many of your negative messages you can recall. Don't be shy. Include them all, even the meanest ones.
- Close your eyes. Listen to the words.
- Visualize those messages as they rise in front of you. Then, one at a time, imagine each negative message floating up into the sky, sailing higher and farther until it becomes a mere speck and disappears over the horizon.

The Mid-Story Crisis

*Thirty years ago my older brother, who was ten years old at the time,
was trying to get a report on birds written that he'd had
three months to write . . . He was at the kitchen table close to tears . . .
immobilized by the hugeness of the task ahead of him. Then my father
sat down beside him, put his arm around my brother's shoulder, and said,
"Bird by bird, buddy. Just take it bird by bird."*

—Anne Lamott, Bird by Bird

SOS!

Women go through menopause and get hot flashes. Men suffer a mid-
life crisis and buy a Porsche. Writers hit the middle-muddle and freeze.
This is nothing new. Even in 1320 Dante Alighieri understood the problems inherent in middles. In *The Divine Comedy*, he wrote about the
Inferno. "In the middle of the journey of life, I came to myself within
a dark wood where the straight way was lost. Ah, how hard it is to tell
of that wood, savage and harsh and dense, the thought of which renews
my fear. So bitter is it that death is hardly more."

Even though Dante is talking about life and we're talking about fiction,
they might as well be one and the same.

THE THROUGHLINE AS LIFELINE

So now you've reached the heart of the book, that painful place where,
like Hansel and Gretel, it's not uncommon to become lost in the dark,
savage wood. It's scary in there. Intimidating. Confusing. The Spoiler
is lurking behind every tree, waiting to grab you as you try to move

forward. It's easy to become frightened and lose your way. But as someone said who must have once found herself in a similar position, "The only way out is through."

The best way to travel the length of your story is to grab hold of the Throughline—the driving force of the book—and refuse to let go. There can, of course, be more than one Throughline in a book. But as you will see, there should always be one fundamental Throughline that pulls the reader from beginning to end.

In Hollywood, screenwriters speak of the Throughline as an unwavering given in a screenplay. They also refer to it as the spine of the story. The Throughline is the central plot point that propels the hero from beginning to end, from one scene to the next, from one act to the next. The Throughline creates the forward momentum that makes the story absorbing and the protagonist spring to life.

Some screenwriters think of the Throughline as the embodiment of the main character's conscious desire. The character knows what he wants and knows that he wants it. This personal hunger, shared by the viewer, drives the story and shapes the narrative.

Somewhere at the closing of the second act of a screenplay, or the end of the middle of a book, the character's conscious desire breaks down. What he wants is denied him, either by his choice or by the force of outside circumstances. This breakdown exposes a deeper motivation that propels the character forward, a motivation he was originally unaware of.

This thirst—this force that motivates the hero and drives the action— becomes a secondary, but equally powerful, Throughline.

Just as a screenwriter constructs a Throughline for his story, an actor constructs a Throughline for his role in a play or movie. As he moves through the play, he thinks of the Throughline as his objective. Each actor has an overall objective, a guiding light he follows throughout the play from beginning to end. Whatever situation in which he finds himself, he does not lose sight of this goal, the Throughline.

The actor also has an objective for each scene—a mini-Throughline, a driving motivation that guides him from the beginning to the end of the scene. It might be as simple as wanting to make a polite exit from a room when the other character won't stop talking or as complicated as trying to divert a character's attention from the dead body in the closet. Either way, the Throughline is there to keep the actor on track, which is precisely what it does for a writer.

The Guiding Light

In Katherine Paterson's *Bridge to Terabithia*, Jess Aarons wants more than anything to be the fastest runner in the fifth grade—"not one of the fastest or next to the fastest, but *the* fastest. The very best."

This ambition constitutes the initial Throughline that defines the overall momentum of the book.

Then Jess meets Leslie Burke, the new girl in school. She's a tomboy and a faster runner than Jess. In spite of their competition, the two forge a powerful and lasting friendship.

Jess and Leslie bond in their defense against a hostile world and their embrace of a world of art and imagination. The two build a magical castle in the woods, a place that can only be reached by swinging over a rain-swollen creek and where Jess must eventually confront his fear of water. "He may not have been born with guts, but he didn't have to die without them."

Beginning with his goal of becoming the fastest runner in the fifth grade, Jess' multi-faceted desire for self-realization becomes the primary Throughline that runs through the story from beginning to end. We see this Throughline manifested in his need to confront his fear and affirm his artistic talent, and we see it in his need to overcome the obstacles life has set before him.

Leslie's accidental death gives rise to the final Throughline of the story. Here, Jess must learn to cope with his grief and believe in himself. Until that point, he was convinced he needed Leslie to "make the magic." Now Jess is alone and must learn to call upon his own creative spirit without the help of his friend. He must also celebrate Leslie's memory by confronting his fear of water and honoring the artist within him.

All of these thematic Throughlines propel the hero forward into and through the action. Each one is powerful in its own right and grows out of the action that preceded it. And each one is presented in a true and spellbinding way.

Throughline in a Nutshell

On a more basic level, in Watty Piper's *The Little Engine That Could*, the story begins with a train carrying toys and food to the good little boys and girls on the other side of the mountain. The desire to make the delivery is the original and sustaining Throughline of the book. The train has toys. The children are waiting.

Before the train can go over the mountain, however, the original engine breaks down, jeopardizing the delivery of toys and food. The dolls on the train ask three engines for help, but they all refuse. Finally, the dolls ask a tiny blue engine, and he agrees to help.

Here, the Throughline shifts from the need to deliver toys to the engine's challenge of pulling the train over the mountain. Will he or won't he be able to accomplish this daunting task? The last third of the story is then propelled by this secondary Throughline, moving from "I think I can" to "I thought I could" in a tale that has entertained and encouraged young children for generations.

Although the focus shifts midway through the story to the new Throughline of finding and receiving help—along with whether the Little Engine will make it over the mountain—the overarching Throughline of the book still remains. Even as we cheer for the success of the Little Engine, we never forget that the boys and girls on the other side of the mountain are waiting for their goodies.

Continuing the train motif, think of the Throughline as a locomotive carrying your main character on the journey through your book. With the exception of experimental novels and other iconoclastic forms, you move down the track in one direction only. You might stop at stations, take on new passengers and let others off, admire the views, even grab a bite for lunch. But always—no matter what—you maintain a forward-moving trajectory. You never lose sight of your goal. You might change tracks, but you don't bring the Throughline to a halt before it connects to the next Throughline or before it reaches the final destination. Even if you employ the liberal use of flashbacks and multiple subplots, the momentum is always and inevitably forward toward your final destination.

From beginning to end, the Throughline is a constant in your story. You can have any number of other things happening in the book. But the matter of what drives the hero and compels him to act is never in question because the Throughline is there to maintain your readers' attentions and to pull them through the story.

Your Turn
Take a Ride on the Throughline

1) Read *Charlotte's Web*, by E.B. White. How does White maintain the Throughline about Charlotte saving Wilbur the Pig? How does he build momentum? Why are you invested in the outcome?

2) Write down how each chapter of *Charlotte's Web* begins and ends. What makes you want to keep on reading? Track the Throughline in the story. How is it maintained in each chapter?

3) Consider your own book. Forget plot for a moment, and think about your story strictly in terms of Throughline. Ask yourself the following questions.

• What is the primary Throughline of my book?

• What are the secondary Throughlines of my book?

• How do these threads intersect?

• How does each contribute to the forward momentum of the story?

• How does each pull the reader through the story?

4) If you can't answer the questions under number 3 with confidence, take the time to think about them.

• Make a list of your Throughlines.

• Devise ways to can make the Throughlines stronger.

• Keep these threads in mind as you write your book, making certain they are fully realized in your story.

Chapter Nine

Classical Drama in the Age of the Page-Turner

One of the few things I know about writing is this: spend it all, shoot it, play it, lose it, all, right away every time. Do not hoard what seems good for a later place in the book, or for another book; give it, give it all, give it now.

—Annie Dillard

Sophocles Revisited

We've already talked about the exciting force in classical Greek drama—the original catalyst that creates the opposing forces of action and reaction. This beginning comprises the opening scenes of the plot in which the booster rockets on the spaceship propel you through the Earth's atmosphere and into space.

Although the structure of classical drama might seem irrelevant when compared to the elements that go into contemporary storytelling, the two are closely related. This Greek drama stuff isn't as outdated or remote as it first appears; an understanding of this structure will help you in all your story-telling efforts.

Basic Dramatic Structure

According to *A Handbook to Literature* by William Flint Thrall and Addison Hibbard, classical dramatic structure is divided into distinct, identifiable parts.

1) The Rising Action

    a) exciting force

    b) conflict and complications

2) Climax

3) Falling Action

    a) the reversal

    b) the resolution

    c) the last moment of suspense

Imagine these elements as a triangle with the climax at the peak. When represented visually, scholarly types call this Freytag's Pyramid, named after German playwright and literary critic Gustav Freytag, who devised this chart in 1863.

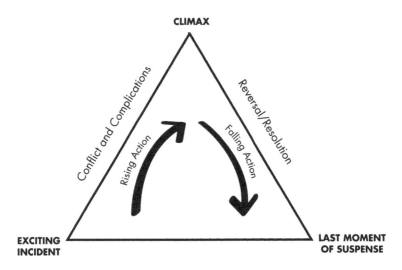

Whether the classical Greek dramatist was dealing with comedy or tragedy, these critical story elements did not change. Twenty-five hundred years later, this structure is still useful.

Although I trust you're not going to be writing a mother-son drama called *Oedipus Goes to Kindergarten*, looking at your story from this classical point of view is one possible way to move you out of your middle-muddle rut and help you envision your plot from a different perspective.

Keep in mind that the middle of your story moves through the conflict and complications, the climax, and the reversal and resolution.

Suppose those exciting force booster rockets were powerful enough to propel you through the Earth's atmosphere and into outer space. You're on the way to a quiet vacation on the Moon, and you're now entering the middle of the journey, the longest and most dangerous part of your fictional odyssey. Lots of things can go wrong here—batteries die, directional signals get screwed up, space suits leak—and it is your job to keep all the parts tuned and in working order so you can overcome the obstacles you confront, complete your mission and reach your destination.

Rising Action

This section deals with the left side of the pyramid—all the action that leads up to the climax.

Exciting Incident. Once again, this is the opening gambit. What takes place here is the catalyst that propels the hero into the rest of the story. Something happens, some incident or conflict or revelation, that sets the rest of the plot in motion.

Conflict and Complications. You've sailed past the gravitational pull of the Earth, and you're hurtling through space on your way to the Moon. This part of your journey encompasses the conflicts and complications set in motion by the exciting force. The most critical challenge of your mission is to overcome the obstacles that prevent you from achieving your goal of landing on the Moon. Here, you are dodging meteors, avoiding asteroids and doing your best to escape dangerous pieces of space junk that fly into your path.

Your journey is a struggle; sometimes it's touch and go. But you manage to survive the asteroid field and space debris, and soon you'll move into the Moon's gravitational pull and glide onto the Sea of Tranquility. You take a deep breath and relax.

Climax

This is the point of highest interest in your story. The emotional peak. The moment where the rising action becomes the falling action.

You've encountered and overcome conflicts and obstacles. Your spaceship has had a close call with an asteroid. You have negotiated the hazards of space junk jettisoned by astronautical litterbugs. You've reclaimed the tether used for space walks. And you've repaired the broken airlock on the lunar module. It's smooth sailing from here on out. Smiling, you glance out the porthole of the spacecraft.

Holy Toledo! You're staring directly at a giant meteor. You and that killer rock are on a collision course!

You shift into emergency mode. Quick as you can, you recalculate your trajectory. You fire your directional rockets, but nothing happens. The meteor keeps coming straight at you.

Desperate, you fire the rockets again in one last attempt to avoid a collision. Just in time, you manage to change your course and avoid certain death.

Whew! You're one of the lucky ones. You miss the meteor. But only by a few inches.

Falling Action

This section deals with the beginning of the resolution, all the action that happens after the high drama of the climax.

Reversal. You sigh with relief. You've escaped a fiery death, and you're finally headed for a soft landing. You sit back and relax. Suddenly you realize that because you had to recalculate your trajectory to avoid the meteor, your current course is going to hurtle you past the Moon and into the endlessness of deep space!

Terrified, you revamp, recalculate and reset your course.

Your efforts pay off. You move into the Moon's atmosphere and into its gravitational pull.

Resolution. Finally, after coping with major crises, confronting mortal danger and overcoming numerous obstacles, you land safely on the Moon.

Last Moment of Suspense. This moment comes when all the plot points are resolved and suddenly there's one last reason for pause. Oh dear! Did you remember to pack the picnic lunch in the spaceship? It's in the basket by the door. But wait! The exit door is locked. Where are the keys? Ah, yes. In your pocket. You've now got everything you need for a quiet and restful vacation.

Given the fact we're not writing an actual Greek tragedy in which the hero overcomes all obstacles in his path only to discover he has inadvertently committed a hideous, horrific and unforgivable sin, we'll shift into the resolution and skip the classical denouement in which the hero comprehends the horror of his act, gouges out his eyes and is condemned to wander forever as a blind man and a beggar. Not the stuff of which fourth-grade fiction is made.

The main point to understand about classical structure is that as you write your story, you can use the plot points to work toward preset goals. One stage of the drama unfolds into the next in a kind of organic whole. Each element of your story grows logically out of what has come before.

You move in a deliberate and calculated way from exciting force through conflict and complications to climax, then on through reversal and resolution to the last moment of suspense. What you add to this plot—your creativity and unique point of view—is what makes your story interesting and your book exciting to read.

WILD THINGS IN CLASSICAL DRAMA

Lest you be tempted to dismiss this structure as old-fashioned and irrelevant, let me assure you that the concepts of classical drama aren't just abstracts that have no practical application for storytellers today. Whether we're talking about a complicated YA novel or the fundamentals of a picture book, the principles of classical drama can help structure your story and move your action forward to its logical, organic conclusion.

Consider, if you will, *Where the Wild Things Are.*

Rising Action

Exciting Force. In this story, the exciting force begins the night Max wears his wolf suit, makes mischief and talks back to his mother. This naughty behavior sets the story in motion. The hero is sent to his room without his supper and is thus propelled into the heart of the drama.

Conflict and Complications. Once Max is in his room, the forest begins to grow all around him and an ocean tumbles by. Then Max steps into his private boat and sails through night and day to where the wild things are.

The real trouble begins when Max runs into the wild things and must confront these monsters head-on.

The Climax

This is the point of highest interest. Here, the wild things roar and gnash their teeth and roll their eyes and show their claws. Max stands up to all the monsters and learns to tame them with a magic trick. Once he has accomplished this feat, Max proclaims that the wild rumpus should begin. And so Max and the wild things cavort together as they howl at the moon and swing from the trees.

The Falling Action

The Reversal. In the reversal, Max sends the wild things off to bed without their supper. But once the monsters have disappeared, he realizes he's lonely, and he wants to go home.

The Resolution. Although the wild things beg Max to stay, he gets into his boat, sails toward home and arrives safely in his room.

Last Moment of Suspense. Oh dear . . . Is Max's mother still angry? This anxiety is alleviated when our young hero finds his supper waiting for him. In fact, the food is still hot.

So there you have it: children's literature as Greek drama. Whether you're a novice writer or a published author, the elements of classical structure offer you the framework to give your story direction and the plot points to give your hero forward momentum.

THE PAGE-TURNER VS. THE HO-HUM READ

When I first started writing, I took it upon myself to figure out what it was that made me want to keep on reading—what qualities created a page-turner and what techniques contributed to a riveting read.

Since I didn't know the first thing about writing, I decided to dissect a book that didn't let me put it down. A big-time, gotta-read-it, 3 A.M., can't-close-the-covers page-turner. In this case, I chose Mario Puzo's *The Godfather,* a book I had read but never analyzed.

For the first time in my writing life, I read a book for strictly technical reasons.

In film, a musical theme or song for the next scene often starts playing before the previous scene ends. A technique first used in a movie called

The Graduate, the song pulls the viewer forward into the story, connecting one scene to the next with a melodic thread that creates a musical momentum all its own. Puzo does something similar in *The Godfather*. The author structures his story so he wraps up one story line in the middle of one chapter and begins another that doesn't end until the middle of a future chapter, 50—or 250—pages down the line.

Obviously, Puzo didn't invent this trick. When Charles Dickens wrote *Oliver Twist*, it was serialized in a monthly magazine called . . . surprise . . . the *Old Monthly Magazine*. Each installment was a short, self-contained unit. Yet it also left the reader eager to know what would happen next to Oliver or Fagin or the Artful Dodger. This complicated tale of a young boy running away from the workhouse in which he was born and falling in with a gang of thieves caused readers to mob the newsstands every time the next installment appeared.

In Puzo's cliffhanger approach, the author never ends a "story" at the end of a chapter. Instead, he leaves a major plot line dangling. The reader can't put the book down at the end of the chapter because there's always some urgent need to find out what's going to happen to Fredo, Sonny, Connie or even the Godfather himself. Someone in the Corleone family is always in jeopardy. Or someone who is trying to kill someone who betrayed someone in the Corleone family is in jeopardy. The bottom line is that there's never a moment in the book when you don't want to know what's going to happen next—or in the case of *The Godfather*, who's the next person to swim with the fishes.

You may be surprised to learn that three years before he wrote *The Godfather*, Mario Puzo published a middle-grade novel called *The Runaway Summer of Davie Shaw*, a picaresque story about a fourteen-year-old boy who travels across the country by himself.

The author begins the book with, "Davie Shaw had irresponsible parents, but he was happy anyway." That statement alone is enough to pull kids into the story.

Although his novel isn't exactly a page-turning thriller, Puzo does use a lot of the techniques I've outlined above, injecting a strong sense in the reader of wanting to know what happens next. He ends most of his chapters by posing an implicit question or by implying future trouble that automatically pulls the reader into the next chapter.

For instance, the ending of chapter eighteen creates a natural anticipation of what will happen next: "And tomorrow was Friday, the last Friday in August, the day when his mother and father would check into the Plaza and learn that their son had run away for the summer."

It's almost as if Mario Puzo practiced plot devices on his middle-grade novel that he later used in his opus. You can do this in reverse. The story lessons of *The Godfather* can be directly applied to your early chapter book or your middle-grade novel. You can, however, skip the concrete shoes.

Six Ways to Make Your Book a Page-Turner

1) Evoke Curiosity. Begin your chapter by provoking the reader's interest. Reveal a secret, generate a plot line or create a mystery, making sure these elements have consequences further into the story.

2) Never End at Endings. Avoid ending a plot line at the end of a chapter. That makes it too easy for the reader to put down the book.

3) Think Middle to Middle. Whether you have a short subplot line or an extended one, begin the story in the middle of one chapter and end it in the middle of another.

4) Pose Questions. Construct your chapter endings so you ask a question instead of answer it.

5) Remember to Remind. Keep reminding your reader about the problem your character has, the trouble she's in or the goal she's striving toward that's just out of reach.

6) Honor the Inevitable. Remember that what happens next should be inevitable but not predictable. I'll cover this subject in greater detail in the next chapter.

Your Turn
Embrace the Classics

1) Analyze how the plot points of *Stuart Little* fall into the categories of classical dramatic structure.

• What is the exciting force?

• What actions make up the conflict and complications?

• What is the moment of climax in the story?

• How is the reversal, resolution and the last moment of suspense expressed?

2) Consider your own book, and ask yourself these same questions. Make a chart of the way the plot points in your book correspond to the stages noted on Freytag's Pyramid.

Your Turn
To Turn the Pages

---

1) Read *A Separate Peace* by John Knowles.

• Write down how each chapter begins and ends. What makes you want to keep reading? What character do you find the most provocative? Does Knowles do anything special to pull the reader from one chapter to the next?

• At what point in the story does Knowles begin and end his subplots?

• Track the Throughline in the story. How is the Throughline maintained in each chapter? How does the story lead up to the climax?

2) Now read *Harry Potter and the Sorcerer's Stone* by J.K. Rowling.

• Take particular note of how each chapter begins and ends. How do the last two sentences of chapter three ("The whole shack shivered and Harry sat bolt upright, staring at the door. Someone was outside, knocking to come in.") pull the reader into the next chapter?

• How does Rowling use the "Six Ways to Make Your Book a Page-Turner" listed on page 74?

CHAPTER TEN

Journey's End

Begin at the beginning . . .
and go on till you come to the end: then stop.

—*Lewis Carroll,* Alice in Wonderland

THE FINAL CURTAIN

Just as it's easier to work a maze backwards, it also helps to know what and where your ending is when you begin your book.

From the moment you conceive your opening sentence, you will write with more confidence and move forward with a stronger sense of purpose if you have a general idea about how your story will end. It's not necessary to focus on the fictional destination with every word you write. It's a matter of maintaining a general awareness of your ultimate goal.

You don't need to know all the details of the ending. Nor do you need to know how every step of the final scene will play out. But it's a good idea to have a strong sense of the general direction in which you are going. Setting your sights with this literary compass is a solid way to avoid getting lost in the dark woods. It's also a way to maintain a steady forward momentum throughout your book.

The first thing to keep in mind about your ending is that it must honor the contract you made with the reader in the opening paragraphs. This does not mean the ending must be predictable. But it does mean that the ending must be inevitable.

When art students learn to draw, they are taught perspective. In order to indicate near and far, a road made up of two ostensibly parallel lines grows narrower as it moves toward the horizon line. Think of your story as that road and the ending of your story as the precise point at which the two parallel lines meet. In order to convey the full depth and distance of your picture, the convergence of the lines brings the story together at one final, inevitable point.

THE FUNDAMENTALS OF ENDINGS

There are lots of ways to end a book—from happy, sad and mysterious to ambivalent, comic and tragic. But when it comes to endings, the bedrock issue to bear in mind is to keep the promise you made to your reader at the beginning of the book.

Whatever ending you choose, you must lead up to it in an honest way. Like Hansel and Gretel, even in the simplest story you must have dropped enough crumbs for the reader to follow so the ending is a logical outgrowth of the path you have traveled through the book. In other words, you can't spring a surprise on the reader at the last minute that you haven't laid the groundwork for in advance. Whether you're writing a drama, a coming-of-age story, a thriller or a mystery, you must drop crumbs that lead to the inevitable ending. The groundwork might be obscured and the hints might be subtle, but the clues must be there in order to justify the surprise you create.

Keeping Your Promise

Critical to the understanding of the ending is the understanding that if you've made a promise to the reader, it's your obligation to deliver on it. Anything less than a full payoff is a violation of the author-reader contract.

- If you promise a mystery, end with the solution.
- If you promise action, end with resolution.
- If you promise sin, offer redemption.
- If you promise confusion, end with understanding.
- If you promise anguish, end with relief.

• If you promise humor, end with a punch line.

• If you promise a coming-of-age story, end with insight and growth.

• If you promise a love story, end with a resolved relationship.

The ending of your story should be the inescapable outcome of the plot lines you have woven together throughout the book and the promises you have made. And it should be played out onstage in full dramatic regalia.

Different Strokes for Different-Aged Folks

In children's fiction, the endings of books vary with the age of the reader. Some readers require certainty; others don't. It all depends on the kind of book, the subject matter and the age of the reader.

1) *Traditional Picture Books.* With little children, the way stories are resolved is critical. The endings of the more serious stories offer comfort and closure to fragile psyches. Little children need to feel safe, to feel protected from the vagaries of a capricious world. Time enough for them to learn about unpredictability and its messy aftermath.

It's no accident that fairy tales end with "And they all lived happily ever after." Endings such as this give children a sense of security, a feeling they can cope with the circumstances they confront in their daily lives. Robert Browning expresses this sentiment perfectly in his poem "Pippa Passes": "God's in his heaven—All's right with the world."

Max arrives home and his supper is still hot.

In lighter picture books, humor plays a major role. There's often a twist to the tale, a gentle tweaking of the world in which the characters cavort. Never underestimate a small child's ability to "get the joke." Presented properly, humor evokes a giggle and creates a quiet sense of satisfaction in the reader or listener.

In Dr. Seuss's *The Cat in the Hat*, the mother leaves her two children staring out the window on a rainy day. Everything is quiet and orderly. Then the cat comes along and creates chaos. Before he leaves, the cat cleans up the mess. And when the mother comes home, everything is perfectly tidy again. The story ends with the question,

Well . . .
What would you do
If your mother asked you?

2) Easy Readers and Chapter Books. Again, these stories end on a comforting note. There are no developments left dangling. All's well that ends well. The readers of these books are still fragile, still searching for the signposts in life that allow them to negotiate their way through the increasing challenges of a confusing world. They, too, need to know that things turn out all right.

At this age level, most stories deal with subjects kids can relate to in their daily lives. In their search for security in a larger world, children this age count on the fact that a satisfying ending awaits them.

If you've written a humorous story, it's important to give the ending a clever comic twist, such as the revenge of the slimy, versatile critters in David Greenberg's *Slugs*. Kids love this kind of reverse-situation humor.

Usually, these endings aren't full of laugh-out-loud yucks. A gentle get-the-joke humor is what most of these books aim for.

In *No Tooth, No Quarter*, Jon Buller and Susan Schade find the balance between humor and satisfaction in their story about a boy named Walter who loses his tooth then saves it in his pocket in order to give it to the Tooth Fairy. But, he later explains in an apologetic note to this capricious night visitor, the pocket had a hole in it, and he lost the tooth.

That night the Tooth Fairy—who is already in trouble for handing in a dog tooth, a fake vampire tooth and a cracked tooth with a filling—reads the note and informs Walter that she can't give him his quarter unless she has the tooth. After a trip to Tooth Fairy Land and a useless plea to Queen Denteena, Walter finally cuts the pocket from his pants and trades it for his quarter.

"Will you wake me up when you come for my next tooth?" Walter asks the Tooth Fairy.

"Sure," the Tooth Fairy tells him. "Only try not to lose it before I get here."

3) Picture Books for Older Kids. In the olden days, picture books were geared toward little kids. That's not true anymore. Today some picture books are written for kids up to eight or nine years old and deal with difficult subjects and serious themes.

Florence Parry Heide's *Sami and the Time of the Troubles* takes place in Beirut during the war. And Margaret Wise Brown's *The Dead Bird* examines the ramifications of death when some children discover a dead bird. In this simple but powerful book, the children learn about the finality of death and the necessity of saying farewell as they find a place in the forest to bury the bird amidst ferns and flowers, ritual and remembrance.

Obviously, picture books for older children are more complicated. They aren't required to have a happy ending. But as Janet Zarem, the distinguished children's book consultant, says, "If you can't leave them happy, leave them hopeful."

4) Middle-Grade Fiction. When writing for nine- to twelve-year olds the endings don't have to be happy, but they do have to be satisfying in some fundamental way. In younger books, stories deal primarily with situations and feelings the child might encounter. Here, stories grow out of the characters, their internal changes, and their ability to understand and cope with the world around them. As a consequence, the endings to these books are more complex.

For instance, sometimes life doesn't turn out the way the hero wants it to. Yet she does get some of what she needs—an understanding of how the world works, perhaps, or a new-found ability to cope with a confusing and challenging event. She might have to accept adverse circumstances or even mourn a deep loss. But in all of these situations, the hero learns something. She changes, grows and begins to get a firmer grasp on the complexity of the world around her.

In *Bridge to Terabithia*, Jess Aarons must cope with the death of a friend. And in doing so, he learns to appreciate the invaluable gifts she gave him. In spite of Leslie's death, by the end of the book the hero has grown in courage and vision and creativity.

5) Young Adult Books. By their teen years, kids have developed a high tolerance for ambivalence. They may rail against the fact that their world isn't painted in black and white. But by now they've absorbed the message that things don't always turn out the way they want them to, that conflicts are often beyond their control and life isn't always fair.

Personal challenge and internal change are hallmarks of books at this age. So is a somewhat dark vision of the world. The perennial popularity of the anonymous *Go Ask Alice*, S.E. Hinton's *The Outsiders* and Louis Sachar's *Holes* attests to this. Death, loss and existential angst color the endings of many YA books in shades of gray. "Sadder but wiser" is the phrase that springs to mind.

Given the angst teenagers experience when their hormones are raging and their lives are chaotic, it's no surprise that the endings of their books are often ambivalent. What *is* a surprise is that young adults embrace this irony and ambiguity so readily.

The Ending as Beginning

As certain and inevitable as the ending of a book should be, this does not mean the story stops there. You should do everything you can to convey a sense that the story will continue after the reader closes the book. A believability in the future of the characters is one of the primary elements that makes a book memorable.

In middle-grade and YA fiction, especially, you have created characters who live and breathe, love and hate, rage and submit, avoid and desire, embrace and deny, coax and bluster . . . characters whose lives are lived out in all their multiple manifestations and contradictions between the pages of a book. What they were doing before the story began will continue after the story ends. The circumstances of their lives may have changed. The courses of their lives may have shifted direction. They may have grown in understanding and depth and character. But they will continue to live in ways that the reader is invited to imagine.

After going to summer school and special classes, Lucy raises her SAT scores by 250 points and gets into the college of her choice. But after the story ends, will she overcome the remaining obstacles in her path in order to succeed in the wider world?

Will Rawlf become the man his father wants him to be? Or the man he wants to be?

Will Ben's wish come true and Noah's ambitions be realized?

If you structure your endings skillfully, these questions remain in the reader's mind long after the door is closed on your story.

Readers will embrace your book—and often want to read it again—if you give them the impression that the story doesn't end when it ends. Characters continue to grow and lives continue to evolve. This sense of future possibility creates the longing to know more—the sense of hope that extends beyond the back cover of your book.

In *Mom, the Wolf Man and Me*, Norma Klein ends her story with:

> "So, a new life is beginning for you," Wally said, sneezing.
> "Here's to a new life!"
> Walking downstairs again, I wondered if he was right.

There's no question this story is going to move forward, no question the hero will do her best to live life in the new direction that was set during course of the story.

That's what makes the ending satisfying and the book worthwhile. And what makes readers come back for more.

BEYOND THE END TO THE SEQUEL

Not everyone can write books with an ending that is, in fact, a beginning. Not everyone can write with enough clarity and confidence to herald the coming of the next book. J.K. Rowling is a master of this technique in her Harry Potter stories. The astonishing success of this series is not only a testament to the author's talent and vision. It is confirmation of the fact that children are willing to follow a character through the next book if the previous book leads them to it with skill and intrigue.

In *Harry Potter and the Sorcerer's Stone*, Rowling ends her story with:

> "I hope you have—er—a good holiday," said Hermione, looking uncertainly after Uncle Vernon, shocked that anyone could be so unpleasant.
>
> "Oh, I will," said Harry, and they were surprised at the grin that was spreading over his face. "They don't know we're not allowed to use magic at home. I'm going to have a lot of fun with Dudley this summer. . . ."

There's a distinct sense that some naughty fun awaits the hero. Even if he's not allowed to use his new magical power, Harry is confident he knows how to avoid being a victim at the hands of the wretched Dudley. Needless to say, readers want to share this experience with their hero and to learn how his next year at wizard school will play out.

In Philip Pullman's absorbing fantasy *The Golden Compass*, the author creates a poetic and lyrical tale of classic depth and breadth. The heroine, Lyra Belacqua, is drawn into a world where mystery reigns, hideous things happen and momentous struggles take place. In a masterfully written story that appeals to both adults and children, Pullman deals with complex and provocative subjects—with life and death, truth and reality, good and evil. He ends this first book in the *His Dark Materials* trilogy with Lyra speaking to her companion—her daemon.

"I reckon we've got to do it, Pan. We'll go up there and we'll search for Dust, and when we've found it we'll know what to do."

Roger's body lay still in her arms. She let him down gently.

"And we'll do it," she said.

She turned away. Behind them lay pain and death and fear; ahead of them lay doubt, and danger, and fathomless mysteries. But they weren't alone.

So Lyra and her daemon turned away from the world they were born in, and looked toward the sun, and walked into the sky.

This is an irresistible ending, one that ties up one story as it creates anticipation for the next. A perfect model to look to when you're writing your own series.

PITFALLS AND POTHOLES AT THE END OF THE ROAD

Sometimes when we write a book, we commit ourselves to an ending that doesn't work. We've constructed a story that has one inevitable conclusion, but by the time we've actually written the story, it becomes apparent that the previously planned outcome is a mistake.

As much as I talk about the necessity of the inevitable ending, you should be prepared to change it if your story leads you in a new direction. Sometimes characters and circumstances force you onto a different path—one you hadn't planned, but one that is ultimately more intriguing and appropriate. When detours happen, the most important thing to remember is not to shy away from rethinking and rewriting your story to accommodate the new ending.

U-Turns and Detours: A Personal Aside

Every time I make a major revision, I remember the six full drafts of my first novel I typed out on my trusty Smith Corona portable typewriter. Each draft represented at least three or four weeks of rewriting and typing. That didn't include all the literal cutting, pasting and constructing of new pages with scissors, scotch tape and a copy machine. Compared to the old method, computers make revisions a snap. Cut, paste, insert, rewrite—no scissors or tape required.

Not long ago I was ghostwriting a book, and in the final, down-to-the-wire edit I realized the outline I had followed so carefully no longer made the sense it did when I began the project. The person for whom I wrote the book kept giving me new material that hadn't been factored into the initial outline. These contributions changed the approach I had originally conceived. The deadline was three days away, and the manuscript suddenly felt overly complicated and confusing.

Instead of crawling under my blankie and hiding (which I was sorely tempted to do), I sat down at my computer and spent three intense days reconfiguring the entire book. I eliminated old chapters and sections and created new ones. I cut and I pasted, then rewrote old text and tied it all together with new text that bridged the gaps I had created.

I couldn't have done this on a typewriter; it wouldn't have worked. I would have bowed my head and resigned myself to handing in a book that wasn't as good as it could have been.

With the help of a computer, serious, sweeping revisions are always possible. You should never shy away from them. Nor should you think they are not worth the effort.

No matter how hard or painful the work might be, improving your manuscript is always worth the effort. That said, however, I would emphasize there's a good chance you can spare yourself this rewrite trauma if you acquaint yourself in advance with the pitfalls you can encounter at the end of your book. If you put in the effort now, you'll save a lot of time in rethinking, replotting and rewriting later on.

Four Hazards at the End of the Road

At the end of your narrative journey, there are several road hazards to look out for as you travel along the home stretch. Considering these issues in advance can save you time, anguish, and trouble as you wrap up your story and end the fictional lives of your characters.

1) *Dead Ends.* Two years ago I was asked to edit a YA novel that had been commissioned by a publisher. As I read the story, I edited the prose for precision and clarity, tracked the plot and the subplot, and

made notes in the margins, notes for a critique and notes in my head. I also followed the progress of the hero, who was on an ostensible journey toward personal authenticity. By the time I reached the end of the story, I didn't care whether the hero succeeded or failed. I felt as if the publisher and I had wasted a lot of time—and in the publisher's case, money—on a story that didn't work on any level.

At the beginning of the story, the hero wants to go to a special ski resort where his mom and dad don't want him to go. So he lies to his parents in order to get there. Without a trace of a guilty conscience, the hero travels to the resort, sees his friends, has some adventures, gets into trouble, has his driving emotional problem solved for him by someone else and returns home. At the end of the book—since his lie goes undetected—the hero tells another lie to his parents in order to travel somewhere else he's not supposed to go.

The hero has learned nothing. He hasn't grown or changed. He lacks essential integrity. He'll do anything to get what he wants. He's still a shameless deceiver. So at the end of this novel, why in the world would any reader care about him? And why in the world would someone choose to read another book by this author?

The answer is, they wouldn't.

It's probably not a surprise to learn that, ultimately, the decision was made not to publish the book.

I offer this editing saga as an example of just about everything you can do wrong in a story. The hero is dishonest, and it's hard to cheer for the success of a liar. The hero gets into trouble, and someone else gets him out of it. Furthermore, the hero doesn't have enough conscience or insight to understand he's done anything wrong.

Beyond those obvious failings, the author constructs a totally unsatisfying ending. If the hero hasn't grown or changed or learned anything, there's not an ending in all of literature that could convince me this novel is worth reading.

At the beginning of the book, once the hero lies to his parents, the implicit contract with the reader states that he will learn something from his mistake. He will grow. He will change. The hero will learn that deceit has its price. Everything points toward that ending, but the author ignores the signs. This leaves the reader feeling angry and dissatisfied and determined never to read another book by this writer.

• *Ending rule #1:* If the hero doesn't change or grow or learn something important, create a new ending or don't write the story.

2) Speed Demon. One sin that many writers are guilty of is ending a story too abruptly. I've seen it time and again. You make your way through a wonderfully constructed, artfully paced novel, only to have the author tie up the ending in two pages. The reader is left with a sense of "Huh? What happened to the ending? Where did it go?"

Now you see it, now you don't.

This fictional sin isn't uncommon. I suspect the reason this happens is that the author just grows tired of writing the book. He's busted his fictional rear for a solid year, and he's understandably weary. Patience is not the only thing that wears thin on an arduous and demanding journey.

I recently edited an outstanding YA novel that was both intriguing and memorable. But when the author reached the end of the story, he tied up all the loose ends in a flash. Even though the hero was forced to overcome one dreadful thing after another that had been perpetrated by the villain of the story, he never confronted the villain in a final, decisive scene. All the action was played offstage, depriving the reader of the satisfaction of watching the hero stand up to his nemesis. It was as if the author couldn't write one more scene with this character so he tossed the balls in the air and caught them all at once, wrapping up the story in one page.

Which brings me to the moral of this story.

Telling the reader what happened in an abbreviated flashback or exposing the action of the final scene through clever as-told-to dialogue, shortchanges the reader. A poor ending played offstage is no substitute for the full dramatization of your story.

• *Ending rule #2:* You must always play out your ending onstage.

3) Surprise Intersection. Have you ever driven down a road and suddenly come upon an intersection you didn't know was there? Without a warning, the side road appears out of nowhere, and its presence makes no sense.

The same can be said of the amazing coincidence that pops up in a story. Granted, life is full of coincidence. But fiction isn't. Furthermore, you can't introduce a solution to a problem from out of left field.

Let's say you are writing a mystery that involves a solution the hero can't solve because he doesn't know how to lift fingerprints off a windowsill. So three-quarters into your book, when the villain is about to get away with his dastardly deed, your hero runs into a long-lost friend who just happens to know all about fingerprints. By using this coincidence instead of having the hero himself learn about fingerprints, you've just blown the story into disjointed little bits. Again, Charles Dickens might be able to get away with this, but we ordinary mortals cannot.

• *Ending rule #3:* If you haven't prepared the reader in advance for the amazing coincidence, you're not allowed to include it in the story.

4) The Secret Exit Ramp. In classical Greek drama, when one of the gods was in a major pickle, sometimes Zeus would sweep down to the stage from the wings, pluck the hero from harm's way and carry him off to live happily ever after while cavorting with nubile goddesses in the meadows and peaks of Mount Olympus. This theatrical technique is called *deus ex machina*—literally, "the god from the machine."

Children have used *deus ex machina* for years. Every time they end a story with "And then Tammy woke up and realized everything was just a dream," they're introducing a suddenly contrived, last-minute-reprieve element into their tale.

Another rabbit-out-of-the-hat situation might take place when the villain confronts a hero. Just when things get dicey and the hero is going to be defeated, he reaches into the desk drawer and pulls out a laser sword. But if the reader doesn't know in advance there's a laser sword in the drawer, you can't have the hero use it.

Deus ex machina is the literary equivalent of being saved by the bell.

The lesson here is simple. Never ask the reader to buy an ending that's built around the sudden entry of a savior, whether that savior is a bell, a hero or a beast. Even if you hide them well, you must sprinkle those plot crumbs in the forest for us to follow. Not only will I not buy the last minute entrance of the savior, I'll resent his intrusion into the story.

• *Ending rule #4:* No deus ex machina allowed!

~❦~

Study these road hazards. Make them an integral part of your consciousness as you plan your story. Writing with an awareness of these four rules will allow you to bring your book to an intelligent, inevitable close with minimum plot pain and maximum creative pleasure. And it will make the process of writing your book a positive and rewarding experience.

Your Turn
Closing Ceremonies

1) Read *The Light in the Forest* by Conrad Richter.

• What story elements make the ending inevitable?

• How has the character changed?

• How does the author express that change?

• What question does Richter leave you with?

• What makes the ending inevitable?

2) Read the closing lines from the following books, then answer the following questions.

• Do these endings work?

• Are these endings effective?

• What do you like or not like about them?

• What makes the endings memorable?

• What feeling are you left with?

• Has the author conveyed the possibility of a future story?

• How do you think the story will continue?

From *The Catcher in the Rye* by J.D. Salinger (YA/adult novel)

> About all I know is, I sort of miss everybody I told about.
> Even old Stradleter and Ackley, for instance. I think I even
> miss that goddam Maurice. It's funny. Don't ever tell anybody
> anything. If you do, you start missing everybody.

From *I Am the Cheese* by Robert Cormier (middle-grade/YA novel)

> It's cold as I pedal along, the wind like a snake slithering
> up my sleeves and into my jacket and my pants legs, too.
> But I keep pedaling, I keep pedaling. . . .

From *The Giver* by Lois Lowry (YA novel)

> Downward, downward, faster and faster. Suddenly he was

aware with certainty and joy that below, ahead, they were
waiting for him; and that they were waiting, too, for the baby.
For the first time, he heard something that he knew to be
music. He heard people singing.

Behind him, across vast distances of space and time, from
the place he had left, he thought he heard music too. But
perhaps it was only an echo.

From *The Littles Take a Trip* by John Peterson (early chapter book)

"I'm Tina Small," said a girl to Lucy. "Your brother's in the
house. He's okay."

"I knew you were Tina," said Lucy.

"How'd you know?"

"I don't know—I just knew."

And so began the first annual meeting of the tiny people of
the Big Valley.

From *Man Out at First* by Matt Christopher (early chapter book)

Turtleneck dropped the bat and spun around quickly. He
caught the protective helmet Nick had tossed to him. Nick
laughed.

"Nice to have you back, T," he called from the dugout.

Turtleneck just grinned and picked up the bat.

Okay, Alec Frost, he said to himself. Throw that ball as hard
as you can. I'm ready!

From *Mouse Soup* by Arnold Lobel (early reader)

The mouse hurried to his safe home. He lit the fire, he ate
his supper, and he finished reading his book.

From *Summer of My German Soldier* by Bette Greene (middle-grade
novel)

As Ruth pulled open the heavy front door, my heart felt as

though it was spilling over with so many things I wanted to say, but I didn't have the words for a single one of them. For a moment I thought I was about to call out, "Goodbye," but I didn't. The door closed. And the moment and Ruth were gone.

For moments or minutes I stood there. Not really moving. Barely managing to tread water. Was it possible for a beginning swimmer to actually make it to shore? It might take me my whole lifetime to find out.

Structural
Supports

Scenes

The scene is the basic large building block
of the structure of any long story.

—Jack M. Bickham, Scene & Structure

FORWARD MOMENTUM

Now that we've covered the overall structure of the book, it's time to consider the material that fits inside that structure.

The largest entity of a story is the scene. The basic purpose of a scene is simple: to move the reader from one point in the plot to the next. Think of the scenes in your book as stepping stones that steer you down the path of your plot. Each stone is separate from the other yet each is connected to the other. When the stones are linked together, they not only form a larger whole, they lead the reader from the beginning, through the middle, to the end of your fictional journey.

Some writers view this journey as a process of scene and sequel. Others treat it as action and reaction. Each reaction grows out of the previous action. Each sequel grows out of the previous scene.

Reactions to events come in four basic flavors.

- Emotion
- Thought

- Decision

- Action

One thing leads to another that leads to another.

Just as a book has a beginning, middle and end, so does each scene. Although simple chapter books might only have one scene per chapter, in more complicated stories, chapters have a series of scenes, each one linked to the next.

Some people think of their scenes as mini-short stories. However, there's one important difference between a story and a scene: The short story has a resolution and conclusion, whereas the scene moves the action forward by avoiding these elements.

Instead of resolution, the end of each scene ratchets up the intensity of the story by asking a question or complicating the plot. Instead of conclusion, the scene mires the hero deeper in his dilemma, forcing the reader to move on to the following scene in order to find out what happens next.

To accomplish this goal, James N. Frey, author of *How to Write a Damn Good Novel* and *How to Write a Damn Good Novel II*, says the hero should always emerge from the end of the scene in deeper trouble than when he began.

A Scenic Overview

- The opening of the first scene of the book sets the stage for your story.

- To begin a new scene, you either pick up where you left off in the last scene, shift to a new situation or move to the subplot.

- In the middle of your scene, the conflict continues to play out or the complication increases. This escalating action is presented either in flashback or chronological order.

- The end of the scene worsens the situation of the hero and points to future action, propelling the reader forward into the next scene.

The Ten Commandments of Scene Sense

1) *Honor the Law of Cause and Effect.* In a movie, when the camera lingers, even fleetingly, on an object, this is a hint to the viewer that

something is afoot. This object is going to play a part in the story. If it turns out that the object *doesn't* play a part, the viewer is left wondering why the director led her astray.

The same concept applies to a book. You cannot present a situation that drops a hint about a possible future action without following up on it. If you create a cause, you must have an effect. Every action must have a reaction.

Readers, including children, are astute. Kids will remember you implied that Andrew's mother will freak out if she finds out about the secret lemonade stand. Teens won't forget that Damon's father is a detective in the drug division of the LAPD, especially if the main characters are smoking dope.

Each of these statements, no matter how casual, demands a follow-up. To ignore them is to break your contract with the reader.

2) Create Credible Motivation. Remember in movies when the novice actor asks the director, "What's my motivation to walk across the room?" We roll our eyes at this silly question, yet attention must be paid to this very issue.

In fiction, characters do not function in a vacuum. They don't suddenly do something that hasn't been foreshadowed or for which the reader hasn't been prepared. Linda can't cheat on her test at school without the author creating motivation for this behavior. Maybe Linda is dyslexic, and nobody knows it. Maybe she couldn't study for the test because she had a fight with her boyfriend. Maybe she discovers her father cheated on his income taxes, so she figures it's OK for her to cheat, too. Whatever the reason—or reasons—for her behavior, sooner or later, Linda's motivations for her actions must be justified.

As you write, ask yourself if your character's actions are credible. Given her background, personality and inclinations, is this action or thought or decision believable? If it is not, either remove the action or rewrite previous scenes to set up this scene.

3) Avoid Dead Ends. When you write your scene, remember that you must move from point A to point B. You cannot begin at point A and finish in the same place at the end of the scene. If the action hasn't moved forward, the scene doesn't belong in the book.

There are two basic ways to avoid a dead end.

• *Point to future action.* If you begin a scene with the hero coming upon a treasure, you can't end the scene with the hero looking through the treasure chest—unless, of course, the hero opens the chest to find the ten-million-dollar diamond that everyone knows was stolen from the mansion on the hill. Some forward action must be implied, otherwise the story remains static.

Is the hero going to tell his parents what he found? Is he going to remain silent and try to find out who the treasure belongs to? Is he going to keep the treasure a secret so he can share it with his girlfriend? Or is he going to call the police? There are lots of possibilities, even the hero's confusion about what to do being one of them. The rule here is to make certain you imply future action before the scene ends.

• *Avoid resolution.* The flip side of this point is to avoid ending your scene with resolution and conclusion. If the hero goes to the police, collects the reward and ties up the mystery all in one scene, there's nowhere left to go with the story.

4) Maintain Credibility. One of the great struggles writers face in developing believable stories is creating plots that grow out of a reasonable premise and characters that behave in credible ways.

In a variation on the kid with the treasure, let's say you're writing a YA novel about a middle-class boy from a small town in Nebraska who goes to visit his grandparents in New York City. One night he looks out his window and sees two men burying a box in the empty lot next door. This kid is no dummy; he knows big city street gangs are tough and ruthless. But instead of telling his grandparents or going to the police, he decides to take on two hardened criminals single-handedly. He follows the bad guys and confronts them. When they object to his unwanted attention, the boy beats the daylights out of them.

Gimme a break. Not gonna happen. Not gonna fly. Not credible.

You cannot introduce a surprise, last-minute "fix" for your story. You must have a credible reason for something to occur, and you must set that reason up in advance. If you want this boy to play superhero, you've got to establish the fact that he has spent the last seven years earning a black belt in Karate or mastering advanced techniques of Krav Maga.

The action in a scene must be a credible consequence of previous occurrences, not the result of the character doing something no sane person would ever do or of a last-minute fix or add-on to the plot.

5) Keep Your Eye on the Goal. Sometimes a scene opens with a dynamite plot point then gets lost in the narrative woods. Failure to move forward in the indicated direction is a fundamental mistake many writers make.

As you write, ask yourself if you are moving steadily toward the end of the scene, the end of the chapter and the end of the story. If you follow too many plot or subplot threads that move in too many directions, you dilute the narrative momentum.

If a scene meanders aimlessly, the reader will lose patience and lose focus. He might even lose interest in the book altogether. Then he'll donate the book to the local library instead of keeping it and recommending it to his friends at school, where the teacher hears about it and praises your story on a special Web site for reading teachers—increasing your sales exponentially and catapulting your book onto the children's best-seller list just below the latest Harry Potter adventure, which then gets you the most prominent children's agent in the business who negotiates a deal for the sale of your next book for fifty thousand dollars that wins the Newbery Award.

That's what I mean by losing sight of your goal.

6) Continue to Remind the Reader of the Central Conflict. Conflict lives in the heart and soul of a plot. If the reader forgets what is driving the hero, she won't care enough about him to finish the book.

It's not good enough to open your story with your character becoming embroiled in a first-rate, complex, mind-boggling conflict. If you do not remind the reader of this complication at frequent intervals and ratchet up the intensity of those complications in multiple scenes, you will lose the momentum in the story.

Suppose Molly's goal in life is to get the lead in the school play. Her best friend Tilly also wants that role. So the central conflict is that Molly is torn between her personal ambition and her loyalty to her friend. Auditions for the play are three weeks away. In the meantime, Molly and Tilly play on the same soccer team, enjoy sleepovers and go to the movies. But never once during these three weeks do they discuss the school play. Never once is the reader reminded of Molly's conflict between loyalty and ambition. At the end, the two girls try out for the play, and they're both so good they are allowed to play the roles on alternate nights.

Ho-hum. Big yawn.

By avoiding the conflict of interests—the rivalry, the jealousy, the fear, the anxiety, the confrontation, the confusing emotions—we cut out the heart of the story, remove the drama from the relationship between the two girls and blunt the reader's interest.

Instead of playing it safe, consider the story-telling lessons classic comic books offer us. Year in and year out, Lex Luthor lurks in Superman's background and the Joker haunts Batman's psyche. Neither the reader nor the fictional hero is ever allowed to forget that a confrontation with the nemesis is waiting just around the next corner. This critical push-pull relationship between hero and villain is what drives the stories and maintains the reader's interest.

A more contemporary example can be found in the Harry Potter books. When our hero is born, the evil Voldemort kills Harry's parents. But when he tries to cast his spell against Harry, the infant's power surprises and cripples the dark lord, saving the wizard world from its dreaded oppressor.

Given this background, there's no doubt in the reader's mind that sooner or later, "he who must not be named" will show up in Harry's life again, eager to destroy the boy that caused him so much anguish.

Like a comic book villain, throughout three long books Voldemort lurks just offstage, toying with Harry and his friends, hovering in the dark corners of their psyches and teasing their imaginations. These recurrent glimpses of evil and brushes with Voldemort's avatars propel the story forward toward an inevitable confrontation between hero and villain. Yet it is only in the fourth book, *Harry Potter and the Goblet of Fire*, that Voldemort actually appears. Until that point we are never allowed to forget the evildoer's presence nor disregard his hovering menace—and thus, never allowed to put the book down until it's finished.

7) Conjure Up Interesting Obstacles. If conflict is the engine that drives the plot, obstacles are the motors that fuel the conflict. The hero's struggle to overcome the obstacles you set before her enlists the emotional investment of the reader. Without the reader cheering for the success of the hero, the story falls flat and becomes a bland reading experience.

Going back to Molly in the school play: Instead of competing for the starring role with her friend, suppose Molly has a speech impediment. She's been working with a speech teacher and wants to prove to her friends and family that she can stand onstage and speak without stuttering.

When Molly's classmates hear she's going to audition, they tease her by saying, "Gggg-ood l-lllluck." When her parents hear what she's about to do, they gently suggest she try soccer instead. When her best friend hears about the audition plans, she tries to save Molly from embarrassment. But in spite of all the roadblocks, Molly perseveres. She overcomes one obstacle after another and in the end prevails. She recites her lines perfectly without hesitation.

On the other hand, the story might conclude with Molly repeating her lines with a stutter. In this case, the triumph then lies in Molly finding the courage to stand up and speak before an audience.

Molly overcoming the obstacles, not her desire to act in the play nor her triumph on opening night, is the action that fuels the story.

Set up your scenes so obstacles are confronted in one scene but not resolved until future scenes. This kind of literary steeple chase—jumping over a puddle here and a hurdle there—is what keeps the plot moving forward and keeps the reader's interest from flagging.

8) Use the Two Steps Forward, One Step Back Rule. Just because the hero makes discernable progress toward his goal in one scene, don't allow him to move forward unimpeded in the following scenes. Overcoming one obstacle after another without a setback makes for dull reading.

For instance, even though he's one of the smallest kids in the ninth grade, Hyungkyu's ambition is to compete in a cross-country race between his school and its arch rival in the League Finals. When Hyungkyu appears for tryouts, the coach almost dismisses him; then he sees Hyungkyu run. The boy barely makes the cut. Three weeks into the season, Hyungkyu sprains his ankle.

Two steps forward, one step back.

Hyungkyu works out, strengthens the tendons in his ankle and learns to run with a brace on his foot. Just as he's back up to speed and earning the attention of the coach, Hyungkyu's father develops prostate cancer.

Another step back.

All the way through the climax of the book at the race for the League Championship, the hero struggles to overcome obstacles in order to achieve his goal. Even as he moves forward, he deals with one setback after another. Hyungkyu's response to these events—his discouragement, his determination, his growth—is what makes conflict interesting and the story worth reading.

9) Simplify Your Scene. Do not use one more person in your scene than is absolutely necessary.

At the opening scene of a book, a group of kids is standing in the playground. Sam says something. Rafi responds. They start to hit each other. Instead of staying focused on the two boys, the focus shifts to the reactions of the other kids. As the fight escalates, Prashant says something, then Annie adds her two cents worth. Dolly tries to talk the boys out of fighting. Jack tries to figure out why the guys are fighting. Etsu steps back because she's afraid. Mary Ann looks for the teacher, and David tries to break up the fight.

This might be typical of a playground fight, but it's not the stuff of good fiction. Who's the hero here? Where should the reader's attention be focused? Are all these kids necessary to the story? It's much better to have the boys isolated in the corner of the playground and tell the story of the fight from one point of view.

When you overcomplicate a scene, the reader is forced to spend unnecessary effort trying to figure out what is happening and why, which character is which, who's doing what to whom, what the purpose of the scene is, and how the story is unfolding. Tracking extraneous complications is not only annoying, it creates an intrusion in the narrative and a break in the reader's "willing suspension of disbelief." The word here is: simplify.

10) Increase the Tension by Raising the Stakes. A playwright ratchets up the tension in a scene when she has two actors confront each other. At first, Rick wants to read the letter Maida is holding because he's curious about who wrote it. *Then* his motivation to get the letter intensifies when he realizes the letter Maida holds contains unkind remarks he wrote about her.

You can approach this scene in a different way if you shift the point of view. At first Maida is merely annoyed with Rick because she's heard he said something untrue about her. When she actually reads the letter, Maida shifts into what my mother used to call a double-dyed duck fit. In both situations, your goal is the same: to intensify the experience by upping the ante and revealing information one piece at a time.

If your character is moving toward a goal and every obstacle he overcomes constitutes the same level of difficulty, the story becomes less and less interesting.

Think of your obstacles as Olympic events. The first obstacle the hero confronts may only rate a "three" on the predetermined level of difficulty. But by the end of the climax, the hero should have vaulted over an obstacle that's a solid and impressive "ten."

Warning!

As you construct your plot points, take care not to raise the stakes too high too soon, or you can't escalate the action to a plausible height when you reach the climax of the story. I once heard about a mystery writer who killed off so many people in so many horrific ways by page 50, he reached the point where there was no kind of credible mayhem he could create, short of dropping a bomb, to top his previous murders. There was no more story to tell. The only thing the author could do was return to Go and start over again, this time with only two victims biting the dust in the same number of pages.

So the lesson here is: Save your finale for the finale.

CONSTRUCTING AND CONNECTING SCENES

It's critical to give your book a good send-off, beginning with the first scene. In *The World's Greatest Toe Show* (the chapter book my partner and I wrote), we pull the reader immediately into the story, dangling the hook on the opening line and sinking it at the end of the first scene. One scene unfolds organically into the next.

The Beginning of the Scene

The first scene of *The World's Greatest Toe Show*—which is also the first chapter—is eight pages long. The opening has a dual purpose: to foreshadow what the book is about and to lure the reader into the story.

The beginning of the scene—one full page of text—is comprised of a mini-flashback, starting with the line I quoted in chapter two.

> The Canal Street Club wouldn't have caused so much trouble if Emily Anderson hadn't saved her father's toe in a matchbox.

This opening sentence immediately creates questions in the reader's mind—the main one being how a toe gets saved in a matchbox. The conclusion, of course, is that the toe has been separated from the father's foot. That established, the inevitable questions follow.

How did the toe get disconnected from Emily's father? How and why did Emily save the toe? What does a severed toe look like? What is Emily going to do with the toe?

A little background is then given about the Canal Street Club and how the principal of the school has announced the kids-only contest for the best booth at the school fair.

Then we move up to the present action.

This is the end of the beginning of the scene.

The Middle of the Scene

The middle of the scene takes up five pages. Here, the Canal Street Gang gather in their clubhouse to come up with an idea for their booth at the school fair—an idea that will earn the most money, allow them to collect the Grand Prize of being extras in an upcoming movie and show up their arch enemies, Bunny Bigelow and Violetta Epstein.

The kids consider several ideas for their booth at the fair—palm reading, a cockroach contest, a bake sale—but they are all eliminated. The club members want something more . . . unusual. After discussing how obnoxious Bunny and Violetta will be if they win the Grand Prize, the kids are determined to come up with something original. But the more they talk, the more discouraged they become.

This is the end of the middle of the scene.

The End of the Scene

The end of this opening scene takes up two pages. Here, the action is moved forward and the hook is set to pull the reader into the next scene.

After failing to come up with a dynamite idea for a booth at the fair, the kids become discouraged. Then Emily Anderson says she has an idea. All the kids look at her as she confesses that the day after her father's toe was cut off in the bicycle wreck, she went back to the scene of the accident to search for his severed body part.

> No one dared ask what everyone was thinking.
> Finally, Billy said in a hushed voice, "Did you find it?"
> Emily nodded solemnly.
> Tulu gasped . . .
> "So what did you do?" asked Billy, his dark eyes shining with curiosity.
> "I saved it," whispered Emily. "In a matchbox."

This ends the first scene and the first chapter, leaving the reader to wonder what will happen next and to ponder such questions as: What does a severed toe feel like? Where is the toe? What are the kids going to do with the toe at the school fair?

To Be Continued

The action from the first scene is continued in chapter two, opening with:

> Everyone in the attic froze. Only the drone of a plane over-
> head interrupted the silence as each kid tried to imagine
> exactly what a toe in a matchbox looked like.

In the middle of the second scene, Emily shows the kids the toe, the sight of which evokes appropriate squeals of horror and delight. At the end of the scene, the club members begin to plan how they'll present their toe show at the fair.

And the Beat Goes On

The story moves forward, pulling the reader into the action step-by-step, building the tension scene by scene. In the climax at the school fair, the escalating prospects of having the best booth at the fair and beating Bunny Bigelow and Violetta Epstein come together in a chaotic finale.

At the end of the book, the kids have a funeral service for the toe before it is cremated in the charcoal broiler. (Donating the toe to medical science and burying it at sea are considered and eliminated.)

With Mr. Anderson standing next to the Canal Street kids—who are still wondering which foot has the missing toe—Billy reads a eulogy he has composed for this solemn occasion.

> *Farewell, farewell, O noble Toe.*
> *Thanks for starring in our show.*
>
> *We'll light your fire and say good-bye,*
> *But as the stars light up the sky,*
>
> *We wish you may, we wish you might*
> *Find a foot that fits just right.*

The last lines of the book end with a two-sentence scene in which we skip to the day after the cremation.

> The next evening, Emily tiptoed into her room and hid a large bag of ashes under her bed.
> Wait till next year, she thought. Just wait.

Scene by scene, all the intrigues and actions of the plot come together. The individual components—the stepping stones on the path to the end of the story—have been joined in a greater and more satisfying whole. And at the end of the journey, the reader gets the sense that the story goes on after he closes the book.

This, then, is how scenes are strung together. Once you understand the big picture, the challenge then becomes how to write each individual scene.

ENTERING THE SCENE

Sometimes constructing a scene presents a special problem. Beginners, especially, find it difficult to move into the action.

When I was working on my first novel, I spent an entire day stewing over an important scene that was going to take place at a party.

I tried opening with the arrival of the first guest. I tried opening with the doorbell ringing. I tried opening with people emerging from a taxi in front of the apartment building. I wrote the scene every way I could think of in order to move my main character into that party.

Around teatime, aching with frustration, I stood up from the desk, stomped out the door and walked down the street to my friend Terry's house. I was banking on her to show me how to get my fictional party going. She came through like a true literary trooper.

After explaining the dilemma to my friend and telling her that every party opener I had tried turned into a colossal bore within two paragraphs, Terry looked at me and said, "But Nancy . . . you don't have to begin at the beginning."

Pause.

"Huh?"

"You don't have to begin at the beginning."

"What do you mean?"

"It's called *in medias res*. Latin for 'into the midst of things.' Instead of beginning at the beginning, you start in the middle of the scene . . . in the middle of the party."

Brain kicks into gear.

Light goes on.

"So *that's* how it's done," I say.

There you have it. Major aha! moment for me. Everything I needed to know about a scene but didn't have the sense to ask. After thanking Terry, I marched home, sat down at the typewriter and opened my scene with the hero planted in the middle of the action in the middle of the party.

This common sense approach may seem obvious to most writers. But as an untutored novice, it was not obvious to me. Once I got a handle on this simple concept, however, my novel moved forward at a much more satisfying pace.

Two Points About the Mid-Party Technique

1) *You Must Play Catch-Up.* It may not be immediately apparent, but if you begin the scene in the middle of the action, in all likelihood you're going to have to play a little story catch-up with the reader.

For instance, I open a scene with Mary at summer camp as she picks up a bow and arrow for the first time. This occurs after Mary has told her parents in the previous scene that she absolutely refuses to go to Camp Mini-Poohbah. Instead of taking tennis lessons and singing campfire songs, Mary wants to stay home and overcome the obstacle I've set in her path.

After plopping Mary down in the middle of camp, I can't just move on to swimming and horseback riding. I have to double back and explain to the reader what happened to make Mary change her mind about going to camp. Did she learn that the cutest boy in class was going to the same camp? Did she decide that learning how to ride a horse was worth deferring her goal? Or did her parents bribe her with a promise of a new scooter or a trip to Bermuda?

Warning!

- Although *in medias res* is a terrific way to create additional suspense, it can grow tiresome if it is overused. Too many mid-scene entrances followed by too many delayed plot explanations become annoying.

- The reader can only wonder about what happened to Mary for so long without losing patience. Consequently, do not depend on this ploy for every other scene.

- Save this technique for your juiciest moments. That way you're delaying the action and increasing the suspense when the reader is most eager to find out what happens next.

2) You Can Delay but Not Deny an Explanation. The reader is owed an explanation of what brought the hero to this point. However, until you give that explanation, the reader is kept in suspense—a distinct advantage of the mid-party technique.

In other words, you don't have to explain immediately why Mary changed her mind about not going to camp. Delaying an explanation is a legitimate way to pique curiosity, increase tension and intensify reader involvement. But you do have to explain eventually, or the orientation of the story and the motivation of the hero becomes obscured.

Scenus Interruptus

Interrupting the forward action—a kissing cousin to *in medias res*—is the perfect way to ratchet up the suspense in a novel.

For instance, you've got Cathy in a bind. She's sneaking out the window and, unbeknownst to this rebellious teenager, her parents are waiting for her at the bottom of the ladder, their arms crossed and their toes tapping.

Let's face it. The reader's going to want to know what happens next.

Cathy's already been warned that if she does a Houdini act one more time, she's going to get packed off to boarding school and removed from the influence of her crazy artist friends who are determined to finish filming their movie so they can enter the state competition for high school video dramas and win the prize of a trip to Hollywood where Cathy will meet her favorite movie star.

So here's Cathy halfway down the ladder. At the bottom, her parents wait to whisk her away to a boarding school where she'll be locked up in a dorm with a matron monitoring her every move.

What's going to happen when our intrepid hero steps onto the ground and turns around to see her parents standing there?

You might be eager to find out what happens next, but you'll have to cool your jets.

Because we're not going there yet. We're ending the scene mid-ladder. We're going make you sweat while you wait for your story gratification.

We have a couple of options here. We can flash back, or we can move to another part of the plot and see what's happening in that neck of the woods.

The Scenic Flashback. Instead of moving the action forward, midway down the ladder Cathy gets scared about what she's doing. She remembers her visit to her cousin in boarding school. That's when we flash back to seven months earlier.

"You may as well be in prison," Cathy had said at the time.

And her cousin had agreed.

Before the flashback to the boarding school, of course, Cathy's about to hop onto the ground at her parents' feet, risking banishment to the very place that so horrified her.

The insertion of this scene with Cathy's cousin forces the reader to move through the fully dramatized flashback before his narrative curiosity is satisfied. He can't discover what happens next until the intervening action is played out. Only then does Cathy turn around and see her parents standing there. Until that moment, the reader is kept in suspense.

• *A reminder:* Don't forget to create a solid anchor for the return of the flashback. Kids, especially, need clarity about where they've come from in the story and where they are in the action.

The Shift to the Other Side of the Plot or Subplot. We end the scene with Cathy climbing down the ladder and her parents waiting at the bottom. And instead of shifting into a flashback at her cousin's boarding school or carrying the action forward with Cathy, we shift to a new point of view and pick up the next scene with Cathy's friends who are waiting for her in the park.

In the meantime, Cathy is left dangling on the ladder.

If Cathy doesn't get to the park in time, the kids are going to leave without her. Then she won't get the credit for the film, and she'll miss out on the trip to Hollywood.

So you get the drift. You double back. You shift focus. You interrupt the main action. And by doing so you increase the suspense and leave the reader with a major question dangling in his head.

Obviously, the more sophisticated the reader, the more complicated the story-telling techniques.

Narrative Continuity

Whatever technique you use to increase suspense, always remember to maintain the narrative continuity of your story by orienting the reader in time and space. Giving the reader a narrative anchor is especially important for younger kids who sometimes have problems tracking plot twists and turns.

Each time you reconnect with the main plot, include a prompt about where you are; a simple reminder will do.

For instance, Yen gets in trouble for passing notes in class. The scene ends with the teacher telling Yen he's going to call her parents and tell them about her misbehavior.

In the next scene, Yen is at an after-school dress rehearsal for the school play. This plot line is inserted into the action after Yen's classroom run-in with the teacher and before the confrontation with her parents—thus creating a touch of delayed reader gratification. Yen is obviously anxious during the rehearsal—an anxiety that reminds the reader she is nervous about how her parents will react when they find out she is in trouble. You can increase reader involvement by noting that Yen's parents are extremely strict. It wouldn't be beyond them to revoke their permission for Yen to participate in the play, even though opening night is just one day away.

When dress rehearsal is over, the next scene takes place at home that evening. Yen sits at the dinner table with the intention of telling her parents they're about to get a call from her teacher. This is the moment to give the reader a continuity hook. You maintain the narrative integrity of the story by beginning the scene with something as simple as, "Still shaken from her confrontation with the teacher, Yen looked at her father and took a deep breath. 'I have something to tell you,' she said."

There are many techniques for story construction, and many more for inventing characters, creating settings and increasing tension. But it all begins at the beginning with the fundamental building blocks of storytelling and the techniques for mastering the scene.

Your Turn
Scenic Exercises

Now that we've examined how to construct your book, we can move on to how to tell your story. But before we get into this, take the time to write some scenes of your own.

Move back to the moment when Cathy climbs out the window. Imagine this action in two different ways. Write the beginning, middle and end of all the scenes.

1) In the first approach, Cathy steps out the window, climbs down the ladder and lands right in the path of her parents. Big oops.

- Write this scene from beginning to end, remembering action and reaction.
- Is Cathy excited at the beginning?
- Is she scared, upset or angry at the end?
- Is she aware of the consequences of her actions?
- What does Cathy do when she sees her parents?
- How does she feel when they confront her?
- What do the parents do?
- What do the parents say?
- How does Cathy react to her parents' anger?
- How do you move the action forward—or stop the action before the climax—so the reader is eager to know what happens next?

2) In the second scene, Cathy climbs out the window. This time, instead of having Cathy step on the ground and confront her parents, stop her descent midway down the ladder. Write a new scene, such as a flashback to the boarding school or the kids in the park, to interrupt the action on the ladder. Then write a third scene, completing Cathy's descent on the ladder.

As you write these scenes, remember that each one should have a beginning, middle and end. And each one should be connected to the other.

Questions to answer:

- Is Cathy nervous?
- Is she calm and determined?
- Is she thrilled that's she's getting away with something?
- How do you show these feelings?
- From whose point of view do you write the second scene?
- How do you anchor the return to the ladder in the mind of the reader?
- How does Cathy react when she sees her parents?
- How does she respond to her parents' anger?

- How is the action advanced from the first scene on the ladder to the second?

A checklist to follow as you are writing:

- Construct your scenes with action and reaction.
- Move from point A to point B to point C.
- Create obstacles.
- Avoid dead ends.
- Eliminate gimmicks.
- Raise the stakes.

Create your scenes in two different ways with two different outcomes. Surprise the reader with parental reactions that do not conform to normal expectations.

Write all these scenes from beginning to end, doing your best to give them life and to pull the reader forward in the action. Above all, remember to leave your reader wanting more.

3) Finally, take what you have learned here and apply it to your own book. Examine each scene of your story. As you read, review the checklist and make certain you've honored each point.

CHAPTER TWELVE

Story and Quest·
Plot and Subplot

A story is a tale with a beginning, a middle, and an end.
It's a quest . . . Whether it's returning to Kansas (Dorothy in The Wizard of Oz)
or killing the witch ("Hansel and Gretel"), this journey is the story,
the plot, the means by which your characters' strengths and
weaknesses are unveiled, his or her lessons learned.

—*Barbara Shapiro*

ALTERNATE ROUTES

Looking at your action through the lens of classical drama is just one way to envision your story. If the pyramid approach doesn't appeal to you, try dividing your narrative into three separate acts or taking your character on the Hero Quest. As you will see, both of these methods can be equally effective when it comes to constructing your story. And both can provide you with an effective, time-tested way to tell your tale.

STORY

In the purest sense, character is story.

What happens to characters—how they suffer and celebrate, how they meet challenges, overcome obstacles and find redemption—is the heart and soul and spirit of story.

Most stories contain an essential core of personal truth, some essence drawn from real life that connects fictional awareness with a writer's direct or secondhand experience. This truth needn't mirror the concrete world. Perhaps it is an emotional truth—a spiritual one—that resonates with the writer and forms the core of a story. Perhaps in the beginning, this truth is an unconscious one, an association not yet fully understood.

It is the uncovering of this truth—the search, the investigation, the examination—that makes a story compelling.

FICTION VS. FACT

Sometimes knowledge of real life is enlightening; other times it's inhibiting.

Several years ago when I was on the faculty of the Big Sur Children's Writing Workshop, a woman read the manuscript of her early chapter book about a young boy's encounter with his eccentric uncle, a story based on real life. The characters were interesting, but the story was flat.

Several writers sitting around the table suggested ways to beef up the story, to inject some life into its essentially dull plot. The problem was, for every suggestion made, the author countered with, "But that's not the way it happened."

Which brings me to one of the most fundamental issues of storytelling. You are writing fiction, not fact. If you are to fashion an effective plot, you must discard the facts as you know them in the service of a larger truth. Taking this risk is the only way to make the leap into a story that reflects the reality you know, as well as the world you imagine.

STORY IN THREE ACTS

When you create story and characters, your challenge is to find a way to fit them into their own unique world. Just as plays and movies do, stories come in three basic acts.

The three-act concept is a variation on beginning, middle and end. Looking at your plot through the lens of three acts is just another way for you to consider the fundamentals of story.

Act I) Problem and Obstacle

In the first act, the hero encounters his central problem. He also encounters the first obstacle to solving the problem.

Act II) Conflict and Struggle

Here, the hero comes face to face with choices that create more conflict. Can he achieve his goal despite this, and despite this and despite this? The plot should have at least three major obstacles for the hero to overcome, each one more challenging than the one before.

Act III) Resolution
In the last act, the hero finds a way out of his dilemma and takes the final step toward resolving his problem.

These three acts form the basis of all your stories. When it comes to how you present your material, there's a lot of fictional wiggle room in which to move. But when it comes to creating the foundation of your story, the three-act convention can serve as a sure and reliable guide for the challenging fictional journey you are about to undertake.

THE HERO QUEST
The Hero Quest rests at the heart of story. This is the universal adventure, the journey—psychological or physical or emotional—that we take in both literature and life when we set out in search of knowledge and wisdom.

In Greek mythology, Odysseus endures seven years of imprisonment and then overcomes a series of perils ranging from the threat of the Cyclops to lure of the Sirens before he finally returns home to his beloved wife Penelope. In the Old Testament, Jonah is cast into the sea and lives in the belly of a whale for three days before he repents and is "vomited out" onto dry land.

Just as Orpheus descends into the Underworld to find his beloved Eurydice, the conventions of the Hero Quest demand that the hero descend into darkness before he walks once more in the light.

Just because these stories originated in ancient tales doesn't make their form irrelevant today. Think *Alice in Wonderland* and *The Runaway Bunny*. Also *Bridge to Terabithia*, *The Catcher in the Rye*, *A Wrinkle in Time*, *The Great Gilly Hopkins* and, of course, *Where the Wild Things Are*. In all of these stories, both simple and complex, the hero travels into the depths in order to find himself. And when he emerges, he is transformed.

In *The Hero With a Thousand Faces*, Joseph Campbell says, "Whether the hero be ridiculous or sublime, Greek or barbarian, gentile or Jew, his journey varies little in essential plan. Popular tales represent the heroic action as physical; the high religions show the deed to be moral; nevertheless, there will be found astonishingly little variation in the morphology of the adventure, the character roles involved, the victories gained."

Campbell goes on to say that "if one of the basic elements of the archetypal pattern is omitted from a given fairy tale, legend, ritual, or myth, it is bound to be somehow or other implied."

Given that this mythic foundation is so prevalent in literature, let's travel with Holden Caulfield as he takes us on a guided tour along the path of the Hero Quest.

The Six Stages of the Hero Quest

1) The Hero Is Called to Action. At the beginning of *The Catcher in the Rye,* Holden Caulfield has just been kicked out of prep school. Confused and disillusioned, he sets out on his search for self amidst the noise and clamor of a confusing world.

2) An Irresistible Force Impels the Hero to Accept the Call. Propelled by the experience of the death of his younger brother and his craving to find meaning in a world of inauthentic, "phony" people, Holden fights with his roommate and then, eager to escape, leaves prep school and begins his journey home to New York City.

3) The Hero Crosses Into the Underworld. Holden takes the train to New York City. But he doesn't go home immediately, not wanting to break the news to his parents that he's been kicked out of yet another school. Instead, Holden checks into a hotel and waits until his mom and dad have received the official letter from the school headmaster informing them of the latest bad news about their son.

4) The Hero Confronts the Greatest Danger and Achieves the Ultimate Truth. Depressed and lonely, Holden wanders the streets of the city. There he meets several people from his past. But nobody can anchor him to a sense of his own reality. Desperate, Holden sneaks into his house and wakes up his younger sister, Phoebe.

In a poignant conversation steeped in the pain of lost innocence, Phoebe asks Holden what he wants to be. He wants to be a catcher in the rye, Holden tells her. He wants to stand guard over little children as they play in a field of rye, to stand at the edge of a cliff and save the children before they fall.

5) The Hero Is Unsure He Can Leave the Underworld. Confused—not knowing where to go or what to do—Holden continues to wander the city. Then he arranges to meet Phoebe in Central Park. In a last nod to his dying innocence, Holden buys a ticket for his sister to ride on the carousel. Later he says he's going to run away, but in his fragile emotional state, this seems unlikely.

6) The Hero Decides to Return to the Upper World, but Is Changed Forever and Cannot Return to Where He Began. Ultimately, Holden goes home and ends up in a psychiatric hospital. While there, he talks about trying a new school and missing the people he used to know. He knows now he will once again enter the world, his innocence lost but his desire to begin a new life intact.

This, then, is the Hero Quest: the journey from innocence to understanding. The search for meaning and the longing for home. The passing through darkness on the way to the light.

As you write your story, conceive of your hero as going on her own quest. Whether you're creating a picture book or a YA novel, you can use the six stages defined by Joseph Campbell as the guide for your hero and the structure for your tale. If you do this, your narrative will be anchored in character and your plot will support your story.

PLOT

Plot is nothing more than the way you organize your story—the way you fit the puzzle pieces together to form a connected and coherent picture for the reader. Whether you use Greek drama, the Hero Quest, action and reaction, or the basic rules of beginning, middle and end, plot is the glue that holds character and story together and that makes the story compelling to read.

Principles of a Strong Plot

Choose One Idea, a Few Characters and a Few Incidents. Don't overburden your story with too many plot lines, obstacles and distractions. If you have a strong character, you can create a textured and complex story within the structure of a simple plot.

Practice Tough Love. Just because you write a scene, you don't have to include it in the book. If a scene doesn't advance the plot or develop the characters, rewrite it or get rid of it.

Create Defining Conflict. At the beginning of the book, make certain the reader understands what the central conflict of the narrative is. This sets up the story for the action that follows.

Use Plot to Translate Character Into Action. When the hero confronts an obstacle, the action that follows is a result of the hero's response to the obstacle. Reaction follows action; action follows reaction. The elements of the plot drive the character's behavior and evoke the responses that define that character.

Remember That Choice Creates Conflict. Without choice, there is no conflict. In literature, as in life, the torment of deciding between two equally weighted alternatives creates one of the most powerful conflicts a character can confront.

Use Obstacles to Pull the Story From Beginning to End. Moving from one obstacle to the next creates steady forward momentum and helps maintain a strong story line.

Write With a Consciousness of Pacing and Tension. In the rising action of your story, you can maintain reader interest by upping the action ante with each succeeding scene. The initial obstacle the hero overcomes must be smaller than the one that follows.

Create Suspense by Creating Limits.

• *Limit time.* If the hero must accomplish his goal by a certain time, day or date, the motivation for continuing to read is automatically built into the story. Will the hero succeed in time or won't he?

• *Limit revelations.* Parcel out pieces of the plot puzzle one item at a time. Parcel out resolutions to the dilemma one detail at a time. Nothing should be solved all at once.

Remember That Action Springs From Character. The way you keep your story compelling and your plot honest is to make certain that whatever your hero does, it comes out of an authentic place. The hero's character dictates the response to the action. Action does not dictate character.

Dramatize the Resolution. As I emphasized in the section on endings, be sure to play out your ending in full and onstage. Anything less cheats the reader.

SUBPLOT

A subplot is a story told in a quieter voice than the plot. Subplots add texture, interest and meaning to the plot. As story-telling devices, they supplement, enlighten and enlarge; they amuse, engage and complicate. The subplot is a way to tell another tale, a way to add interest, increase suspense and enrich your story. The subplot can be a reflection of the plot or stand in opposition to it.

Some stories have one subplot; some have several. The choice is up to you.

As a general rule, try to envision your story as a tale that includes both plot and subplot. This allows you to expand the narrative horizons, enrich the texture, and increase the depth of both your action and your characters.

Notes About Subplot Characters

The Weight Rule. Be sure to give your protagonist the most weight in the story. Never forget that the hero is the most important character, the one to whom the most attention must be paid. The secondary character should never share equal time or prominence with the protagonist. This confuses the reader and leads her astray.

The Scene Rule. No matter how interesting the subplot is, the secondary character should never get as many scenes as the protagonist. If you violate this rule, you risk losing the reader's allegiance to the hero. There is no precise formula for the scene count, but there should never be any question in the reader's mind which character dominates the story.

Basic Approaches to Subplot

There are two fundamental ways to insert a subplot into your story. What method you choose depends on how you want to tell your story. Don't be afraid to innovate and think of new ways to tell an old story.

Weave. This is probably the most common approach to subplot. In this method you integrate the subplot into the plot, advancing each as you go forward. Sharon Creech does this in *Chasing Redbird*, the story of a young girl named Zinny who uncovers a hidden trail near her home at the same time she uncovers mysteries within her own family. Both stories propel the plot forward in an intriguing, interwoven way.

Alternate or Combine. The most basic way to juggle two stories is to set up a plot and subplot and then alternate chapters. This is a cut-and-dried situation, one which kids like because it allows them a clear, in-depth depiction of two points of view.

That said, there are lots of ways to tell two separate but related tales, as you can see in the following section.

Six Strategies For Subplot

Subplots enhance your story in several different ways. Don't be afraid to experiment with unusual approaches. Keep trying until you find the method that feels right for both your plot and your characters.

1) Create a Subplot That Pulls the Reader Through the Story. In Chris Crutcher's *Ironman*, the author fashions two distinct plots for his middle-grade novel. In the primary story, Beauregard Brewster is practicing for a swimming-biking-running triathlon called Yukon Jack. He has also had a run-in with his football coach and English teacher. As a consequence, the teenager has been ordered to attend some anger management group sessions at school.

In the secondary plot, Beau writes a series of unsent but revealing letters to Larry King, the TV and radio personality. The letters not only enhance the story, they provide insight into the psyche and life of the seventeen-year-old protagonist.

The combination of sports and psychology makes this book both realistic and memorable. The epistolary subplot pulls the reader through the plot by the episodic revelation of private thoughts and incidents that add depth and understanding to the emotional and psychological life of the character.

2) Alternate Plot and Subplot. Peter Dickinson uses this technique beautifully in his YA novel *A Bone From a Dry Sea*. He begins with a girl named Vinny who travels to Africa to spend the summer with her paleontologist father. Working alongside a group of archeologists, the two excavate a site that indicates the earliest precursor of man might have been a sea ape, not the land ape that current scientific theory supports.

The novel relates two stories, alternating plot and subplot in separate chapters. The first story is about Vinny, her father and the archeologists as they confront the historical and scientific implications of a unique bone the girl finds. The second story is the tale of the sea apes that once occupied that site. In an intriguing technique that alternates chapters between present and past, Dickinson frames the stories so that each is related to the other and each reflects and sheds light on the other.

3) Weave Plot and Subplot Together. In the middle-grade novel *Nobody's Family Is Going to Change,* Louise Fitzhugh tells the story of Emma, who wants more than anything to be a lawyer when she grows up. Her tradition-bound father roundly objects, carrying this disapproval to his son whose ambition is to be a dancer.

This is the story of two children battling to discover their identities and to affirm who they are. It is also a story about black and feminist rights, family relations, and the pain of being fat in world that stigmatizes everything but thin.

Fitzhugh weaves the plots and themes together with skill, creating a story that is touching and thoughtful in its ability to convey interesting and significant ideas, while respecting the intelligence of the young reader.

4) Use the Subplot for Comic or Romantic Relief. William Shakespeare was a master of using the subplot for comic relief. Nowhere is this better portrayed than in *A Midsummer Night's Dream.* And nobody retells these stories for children better than Leon Garfield in his *Shakespeare Stories.*

The midsummer story begins with the wedding plans of Theseus, the Duke of Athens, and Hippolyta, the Amazon queen. But the plot focuses on Hermia, who has been promised to Demetrius, but who is in love with Lysander. Hermia and Lysander escape together into the forest, pursued by Demetrius and Helena. To further complicate matters, Helena is in love with Demetrius.

In the subplot, the young lovers are discovered by Oberon and Titania, the king and queen of the fairies, along with Puck, the merry wanderer of the night who sprinkles love-juice in the eyes of the star-crossed lovers. This entertaining, amusing subplot of trickery and intrigue lends comedy and romance to the story and ultimately brings about the changes that unite the lovers who truly belong together.

5) Use the Subplot to Reveal the Hero's Character. In the classic *Summer of My German Soldier,* Bette Greene uses the subplot to demonstrate twelve-year-old Patty Bergen's strength, determination and integrity.

[119]

This is the riveting story of a Jewish girl who lives near a prisoner of war camp in Arkansas during World War II. When Patty encounters a frightened young German who has escaped from the camp, instead of turning him in to the authorities, she risks maternal rejection—along with family and community wrath—to hide the young man above the garage.

Patty's recognition of the common humanity between herself and her presumed enemy is a powerful contrast to how she is treated by her brutal, abusive father. This raises the question of who the real enemy is.

Patty's ability to survive the brutality in her family—the subplot—demonstrates her strength and character. These qualities give her the courage to break the law and stand up for the life of this sympathetic prisoner of war.

6) Dramatize the Subplot As a Story Within a Story. In her remarkable picture book *Aunt Isabel Tells a Good One*, Kate Duke opens the action with an artistic bohemian mouse named Aunt Isabel who sets out to tell her niece Penelope a story. But instead of merely telling the tale of villains and romance with a feminist twist, Isabel teaches Penelope how to tell a story—how to construct a plot from the beginning (long, long ago), through the conflicts (the problems, then what happens next), to the resolution (in which the princess overcomes the villain and saves the prince) to the ending (celebration sans nuptials, since career must be established before marriage).

This is a delightful tale in which the present-time story and the story-within-a-story fairy tale both move at a fast and entertaining clip. The plot and subplot enhance and complement each other as they teach and entertain throughout this charming and original fairy tale told with an up-to-date twist.

Your Turn
Establishing Plot Lines

1) Take the story you wrote about a character who goes to meet a stranger. Think about how you want to tell the story, dividing the narrative into three acts. Consider how you want the characters to interact

and how you want the story to progress. Pay close attention to the challenges set forth in each act.

Act I) Problem and Obstacle

Act II) Conflict and Struggle

Act III) Resolution

2) Once you have outlined the book, add a subplot. Decide whether you are going to weave the subplot into the plot, present it in alternating stories with the plot or devise some combination of those two techniques.

3) After you have established both plot and subplot for your story, look at your hero and ask yourself how her story can be adjusted to honor the idea of the Hero Quest. Keep the six steps of the quest in mind as you work on the details for your character's journey.

4) Finally, as you write, refer to the guidelines for story, plot and subplot, remembering that even as these suggestions make demands, they also shape and strengthen the story.

CHAPTER THIRTEEN

The Cast of Characters

*A writer can never know about a character's feelings
what is not somewhere mirrored in her own.*

—Katherine Paterson

MEMORABLE CHARACTERS

As I said in the previous chapter, character is story. Whether you're writing a light-hearted romp, a thriller or a serious drama, how your character acts and reacts—how she thinks and feels, how she handles obstacles and responds to people, places and things—is the essence of story.

If you create a static character, if you do not create a character that lives and breathes on the page, that laughs and cries and makes the reader feel those emotions, no matter how riveting your action is, your story will fall flat.

FROM PLAIN VANILLA TO BUTTER BRICKLE

Like ice cream cones, literary characters come in all sizes, colors and flavors.

When I reflect on the characters I treasured when I was young, I think about Tajar and Laura Ingalls. About Nancy Drew and Holden Caulfield, and even Misty of Chincoteague. These characters are engraved in my memory because they each marked the literary sand with a distinctive footprint. And all these years later I still haven't forgotten them.

There are lots of ways to create memorable characters. Lots of ways to create characters kids can relate to even if the reader is a confirmed city girl and the protagonist is a country boy or an alien or a butterfly.

FIRST IMPRESSIONS

Psychologist Eugene T. Gendlin talks about a "felt sense" we can learn to acknowledge and access when we encounter a specific experience. This is analogous to the visceral response we feel when we first meet a character on the pages of a book. Just as Gilly Hopkins in *The Great Gilly Hopkins* and Maniac Magee in the book of the same name, evoke different sensibilities in the reader, we need to do everything we can to create characters strong enough to evoke their own unique responses.

It's said about people that the first impression is the lasting impression. That statement applies to fiction, too. As far as stories are concerned, this doesn't mean the initial introduction to the main character should be an elaborate happening. Nor does it need to be a whiz-bang, five-star event. But it does mean the introduction should be memorable.

Sometimes the barest beginning can establish a character in the reader's mind. In *Sarah, Plain and Tall*, Patricia MacLachlan introduces her titular character with two sentences.

> Sarah came in the spring. She came through green grass
> fields that bloomed with Indian paintbrush, red and
> orange, and blue-eyed grass.

There's something deeply evocative, almost elegiac, about this simple introduction. We feel Sarah's dignity, and we sense she must bear some sort of resemblance to the land on which she walks. We also sense this is a character we want to invite into our imagination.

On a younger level, consider again my favorite.

> The night Max wore his wolf suit and made mischief of one
> kind or another, his mother called him "Wild Thing!"

We don't even have to hear Max tell his mother that he'll eat her up to know that this is a naughty kid and there will be consequences to his behavior.

At the opposite end of the spectrum, I return to J.D. Salinger.

> If you really want to hear about it, the first thing you'll proba-
> bly want to know is where I was born, and what my lousy
> childhood was like, and how my parents were occupied and
> all before they had me, but I don't feel like going into it, if
> you want to know the truth.

Which of us didn't feel alienated when we were teenagers? And which of us didn't draw comfort from reading about an adolescent who reflected the feelings, if not the circumstances, that overwhelmed us from time to time?

Salinger captures Holden Caulfield in one powerful introductory sentence. Lurking beneath the angst is just a whiff of humor. Maybe it's the use of a word like lousy. Or maybe it's the nakedness of the hero's angst. But I have never known a teenager who wasn't mesmerized by the protagonist of this brilliantly realized novel.

From Eeyore to Maniac Magee, from the Little Prince to Ramona the Pest, the characters who capture the hearts and minds of readers are the characters whose lives are fully realized in the imaginations of writers. Your most fundamental challenge is to know who you are writing about. If you understand the character both inside and out, you can then create someone children want to read about.

LASTING IMPRESSIONS

When you approach your characters, remember it's not just the hero who must stand out. All the characters in your story, children and adults alike, must occupy a unique place in your imagination in order for them to occupy that same status in the reader's imagination.

A Matter of Authenticity

Before you become too involved in writing your story, it's important to establish the essence of your character in your own mind.

A strong character doesn't behave the way you want him to. A strong character behaves the way he should. Every time you write a new scene ask yourself if your hero's action is authentic.

If you're writing about a girl who is excruciatingly shy, she can't walk into a party where she doesn't know anyone and introduce herself to the nearest stranger. A shy girl can't do this unless she's been practicing to take this bold step for months.

Believability is the vehicle that pulls the reader into the story. This means that the actions of the character must be organic, must grow naturally from the heart and mind of that character. Once you have established this foundation, you can move forward into your story.

THE FUNDAMENTALS OF CHARACTER

Kids need to identify with the characters they are reading about. If your reader can't empathize with the character, you'll lose the attention of that reader. You don't accomplish this connection by trying to mirror the average experience of the average reader. You accomplish this by plunging the character into a specific situation.

Your hero can live in the desert, rescue stray dogs, be an alien or pan for gold in the Yukon. It doesn't matter where the hero lives or what he does. As long as the emotions and responses of the character are authentic, the reader can create a bond with him.

There's not a kid alive who hasn't, at one time or another, felt like an alien. There's not a kid alive who hasn't been embarrassed in front of his peers, disappointed in the face of hope or embroiled in conflicts with parents. These themes are familiar, and these feelings are universal. No matter where they take place or under what circumstances they are played out, kids can relate to them.

Beyond the Obvious

It's easy to write about common emotions. Anger, sadness and joy are familiar and accessible to any reader. But try to dig deeper when you envision people you want to write about. We don't live in a black and white world; neither should our characters. Make an effort to paint your character in more muted shades, and don't be afraid to look for subtleties. No need to hammer on a point. Kids are smart enough to pick up on your clues.

How to Create Unique Characters

Validate Confusion. Seek out the confusion in the feelings of your character, the unconscious emotions that drive a kid to behave in one way or another.

After years of hiding from herself, Elizabeth emerges from her shell and revels in her newfound popularity. Finally, she can hang out with the cool group of kids. One day after school she is called upon to choose between agreeing with her popular peers or turning her back on a new girl in class who needs her support. Will Elizabeth do what's right, or will she go along with her friends to maintain her popular status?

Confusion being the hallmark of growing up, there isn't a kid on the planet who can't relate to that feeling of not knowing what to do, of being pulled in two directions at once. Even if a child hasn't been confronted with that specific situation, she has been confronted with the pain of having to make difficult choices. And it is that common bond that pulls the reader into the story.

Celebrate Inconsistency. Contradictions make characters more interesting and readers more involved. This applies to heroes as well as villains. None of us is consistent in thoughts, feelings and behavior. Much as I'd like to have you believe that I'm a woman who's got an intriguing mind, a loving nature and a generous spirit, if you paint me into a corner, I'll cop to the fact that I'm also a woman with a forgetful mind, a reclusive nature and a cranky spirit. So instead of ignoring the contradictions in characters, use them to your advantage.

For instance, create a tough-guy protagonist, a gang member or a similar character. Then have him find a baby bird and, knowing this small and helpless fledgling is unlikely to live, make the decision to feed and care for the bird until it dies. Compassionate defiance in the midst of harsh reality indicates this rough-and-tumble character has the innate capacity to feel pity and the emotional courage to care for a dying creature.

Much as we wish it were otherwise, we're all painted in shades of gray. There's not a human being alive who isn't riddled with contradiction. A girl can treat a kid in the playground with loving kindness, then turn around and treat her little brother as if he were chewing gum stuck on the bottom of her favorite shoes. The intrigue of opposites is what makes the girl interesting.

Warning!

Choose Your Names Carefully

Names are important. They're not something to be considered lightly. Sometimes you might want the name you choose for your character to reflect who she is. Other times you can go for contrast, and the name can reflect who she's not. A regular, average, well-behaved kid can be Jane or she can be Saraphina. A nasty little bully can be named Buck or Ralphie. Each evokes a different response in the reader.

• *Note:* I recently edited a book in which four characters had names that began with "J." Two of them were quite similar. In the beginning, I had trouble telling the characters apart. Was it Julie who made the secret phone call? Or was it Judy?

When readers first approach a story, one of their primary needs is to remember "which one is which." Your task is to help them out. With this in mind, make the effort to give your characters names that can be easily distinguished. The easiest way to do this is have each name start with a different letter of the alphabet. Lina and Lillie aren't as easy to differentiate and remember as Lina and Sarah.

Ignore the Facts. Many of us have written about characters who mirror people we know in real life. Depending on what kind of person inspires you, this process can either be enlightening or inhibiting. If we are intent on reflecting the reality of someone we know, there are two primary issues to keep in mind.

Ignore the Opinions of Others. Often when we create a character, we're inhibited by the fear of what that real-life person—or those people who read the book—will think about what we've written. I'm not telling you to create an exact duplicate of people you know. That would be foolhardy. But I am telling you not to be inhibited by what others might think or say. The writer's craft is full of risk. Creating characters is one of them. As Anne Lamott once said, "Write as if your parents are dead."

Ignore the Truth. As I mentioned in the chapter on creating a plot, learn to ignore reality in order to find the deeper truth. This means you might have to discard or transform what you know. Just because the person on whom you're modeling your character wouldn't say or do something, this doesn't mean your fictional character wouldn't say or do it.

QUESTIONS OF CHARACTER

Creating a sense of wholeness and complexity in your character goes beyond knowing where she comes from, how many brothers and sisters she has and where she lives and goes to school. Character is made up of endless aspects of circumstances, influences, locations, feelings, thoughts, conflicts and preferences. This does not mean you have to demonstrate all these things. But it does mean you should be aware of the multiple facets of your character as you write.

A Checklist for Creating Characters

There are lots of ways to approach the fleshing out of a character. One way to create multiple dimensions in a person who inhabits the pages of your book is to imagine different aspects of that character's inner and outer life. With that in mind, I've created a checklist for you to consider. This is a taking-off point, a framework to help you invent fully rounded and interesting characters. Add to it. Subtract from it. Embellish, embroider and expand it. But most of all, use it.

Personality

❏ Shy	❏ Pessimist
❏ Confident	❏ Optimist
❏ Aggressive	❏ Paranoid
❏ Popular	❏ Underdog
❏ Extrovert	❏ Brave
❏ Introvert	❏ Creative
❏ Risk taker	❏ Logical
❏ Risk averse	❏ Eccentric
❏ Fearful	

Defining Traits

❏ Needs to please	❏ A joiner
❏ Defiant	❏ A leader
❏ Indifferent	❏ A bully
❏ Confrontational	❏ A loner
❏ Cold	❏ A loser
❏ Warm	❏ Disliked
❏ Humorous	❏ Feared
❏ Magnetic	❏ Loves company
❏ Powerful	❏ Seeks solitude
❏ Sensitive	❏ A gang member
❏ A geek	

Origin

❏ City	❏ Central and South America Guatemala, Mexico, Argentina, Peru
❏ Country	
❏ Small town	
❏ Asia Japan, Mongolia, Bhutan	❏ Africa Nigeria, Kenya, Algeria, Egypt
❏ South Seas Australia, Bali, Fiji	❏ America Ohio, Mississippi, Montana, Vermont
❏ Europe France, Austria, Spain, Hungary	

Home

- ❏ City
- ❏ Country
- ❏ Suburbs
- ❏ Island
- ❏ Mountains
- ❏ Plains
- ❏ Desert
- ❏ Coast

Shelter

- ❏ House
- ❏ Shack
- ❏ Mansion
- ❏ Public housing
- ❏ Apartment
- ❏ Farm
- ❏ Ranch

Family Constellation

- ❏ Parents
- ❏ Children
- ❏ Grandparents
- ❏ Stepparents
- ❏ Relatives
- ❏ Married/divorced
- ❏ Relationship with family members

Family Situation

- ❏ Only child
- ❏ Siblings
- ❏ Have single parent
- ❏ Live with both parents
- ❏ Live with extended family
- ❏ Live with grandparents

Best Friends

❑ Same sex   ❑ Mixed

❑ Opposite sex

Interests

❑ Science   ❑ Space exploration

❑ Music   ❑ Movies

❑ Sports   ❑ Math

❑ Food   ❑ Carpentry

❑ Computers   ❑ Inventing

❑ Bugs   ❑ Pottery

❑ Latin   ❑ Reading

❑ Butterflies   ❑ Art

❑ Birds   ❑ Writing

❑ Dogs   ❑ Science Fiction

❑ Cats

Dislikes

❑ Hypocrites   ❑ Piano lessons

❑ Coconut   ❑ Daycare

❑ Brussels sprouts ❑ School

❑ Beans   ❑ Girls/boys

❑ Liver   ❑ Math

❑ Sports   ❑ Writing

Favorites

❑ Music   ❑ Book

❑ Athlete   ❑ Sport

❑ Teacher   ❑ Food

❑ Flower   ❑ Clothes

❑ Artist   ❑ Color

❑ Writer   ❑ Season

❑ Singer   ❑ Subject in school

❑ TV show   ❑ Time of day

❑ Game

Hobbies

❑ Stamp collecting   ❑ Gardening

❑ Coin collecting   ❑ Cooking

❑ Camping   ❑ Painting

❑ Sports   ❑ Sculpting

❑ Model making   ❑ Web site designing

❑ Photography   ❑ Antiques

❑ Politics   ❑ Flying

❑ Computer games   ❑ Parachute jumping

❑ Moviemaking

Pets

- ❑ Gerbil
- ❑ Hamster
- ❑ Parakeet
- ❑ Dog
- ❑ Cat
- ❑ Clam

- ❑ Lizard
- ❑ Iguana
- ❑ Snake
- ❑ Tarantula
- ❑ Ants

Clothes

- ❑ Sloppy
- ❑ Formal
- ❑ Casual
- ❑ Chic

- ❑ Fussy
- ❑ Trendy
- ❑ Old-fashioned

Nickname

- ❑ Name reflects:
  Personality
  Appearance
  Circumstance

- ❑ Hates nickname
- ❑ Loves nickname

Body Language

- ❑ Shy
- ❑ Graceful
- ❑ Clumsy
- ❑ Bold

- ❑ Athletic
- ❑ Defeated
- ❑ Fearful

As you apply these traits, preferences and circumstances to your character, ask yourself the following questions.

- How do the traits reflect the heart and spirit of my character?
- How do they demonstrate who he is and what he stands for?
- What do they say about his inner life?
- What do they say about his outer life?
- How do the traits indicate the complexity of the character?
- What other traits, circumstances or preferences can I include to add depth and texture to the character?

Once you're settled these primary manifestations, it's time to consider some of the finer points of creating a noteworthy fictional personality—a personality that can be a major or a minor character.

Ten Tips for Creating Memorable Characters

1) State What the Character Wants. In the beginning, the character must state what he wants and spend the rest of the story trying to get it. This can be done either explicitly or implicitly.

In *The House on Mango Street,* Sandra Cisneros ends the first chapter of her YA novel with:

> I knew then that I had to have a house. A real house. One
> I could point to. But this isn't it. The house on Mango
> Street isn't it. For the time being, Mama says. Temporary,
> says Papa. But I know how those things go.

Here, the author enlists the reader's allegiance by asking us to take on the hero's quest. We want her to get her house. And we want to cheer her on as she does it. This is the perfect way to pull a reader into a story.

2) Honor Struggle. In the section on dead ends, I talked about the book I edited in which the hero started out lying to his parents and he ended doing the same thing. The character had not increased his understanding, broadened his knowledge nor expanded his self-awareness. From start to finish, he had neither grown nor changed.

Prolonged observation of the status quo is as interesting as watching paint dry. It's the struggle, not the satisfaction, that makes us root for a character and makes a story worth reading. In order to do this, you must begin at a place in the story that leaves the hero room to resolve his problem.

In *That Was Then, This Is Now*, S.E. Hinton writes about a sixteen-year-old young man named Bryon who must come to grips with the fact that his best buddy is a dope dealer. The struggle between being loyal to a lifelong friend and turning him into the authorities is the dilemma that makes this YA novel both powerful and absorbing.

3) Feature One of the Four Fundamental Conflicts. Conflict creates drama and defines character. Without conflict, plot does not exist, you have no story and your character has nothing to overcome. In fiction, there are four basic kinds of conflict a character can confront. Although there can be two or three kinds of conflict in the same story, one usually dominates the plot.

• *Man against man.* In *Best Enemies Again* by Kathleen Leverich, seven-year-olds Priscilla and Felicity have already discovered their dislike for each other in the first book of this series. One girl is prissy and one is a tomboy, and conflict is the name of their game. In the second book, Priscilla once again offers up her trust on the altar of Felicity's deviousness as each strives to get a new bicycle. And once again, Priscilla's innate good nature inadvertently allows her to come out a winner.

For a slightly older audience, *Baseball Fever* by Johanna Hurwitz tells the story of a kid named Ezra who lives and breathes baseball. His father lives and breathes books and chess. The conflict arises because each rejects the other's interest. The quest becomes the search for a common ground that allows each to respect the other's passion.

• *Man against nature.* In man against nature, consider Gary Paulson's *Hatchet*. In this award-winning epic of adventure and survival, a young hero is forced to fend for himself for fifty-four days in the Canadian wilderness after the pilot of the plane in which he is riding has a heart attack. Once the plane is down, the reader's motivation to stay with the story is not only to find out if the hero survives, but how he survives physically and emotionally.

• *Man against society.* S.E. Hinton's *The Outsiders* is a perfect example of man against society. In this coming-of-age story, there are two kinds of people: Socs (socials) who have money and attitude and don't hesitate to use them, and Greasers (outsiders) who struggle to maintain their dignity in a hostile environment. It's us against them for a young gang member named Ponyboy until he witnesses both a murder and a tragic fire. Ultimately, the hero learns this is not a world in which divisions can be made conveniently and in which pain is only experienced by one segment of the population. He also learns there is a place for himself in the midst of this challenging world.

• *Man against self.* Inner conflict is created out of a war between the head and the heart. The conflict becomes most interesting when there is an equal pull in two directions.

The story of self pitted against self is a time-honored literary tradition. Think of Robert Louis Stevenson's *The Strange Case of Dr. Jekyll and Mr. Hyde* and Oscar Wilde's *The Picture of Dorian Gray*. In the award-winning *Eva*, by Peter Dickinson, the thirteen-year-old hero lives in an unspecified but nearby future. One day, she is killed in a dreadful auto accident. Her parents learn that the only way to save what is left of their daughter is to transplant her brain into a chimpanzee. Trapped in the netherland between two beings, Eva is torn between two worlds. Her animal nature and human nature are forced to fight for supremacy—an accurate metaphor for an adolescent trapped in the throes of an identity crisis.

4) Portray Vivid Personalities. This task is easier said than done. Part of the secret of creating vivid personalities is to make characters courageous in their confrontations with their demons and determined in their drive to overcome the obstacles they encounter. This does not mean they are fearless. But it does mean they overcome that fear in order to step up to the plate and be counted.

Ramona the Pest is a standout character. So is Maniac Magee. One of the things that makes these kids so interesting is their willingness to take on the world. They are fierce. They are not afraid to be different. They make demands on themselves and the people around them. And they are determined to change what they see as wrong.

In *The Great Gilly Hopkins*, Katherine Paterson creates a gutsy hero who refuses to accept what life meted out to her. In the beginning, Gilly—a lifelong foster child shunted from place to place—lives under the continuing delusion that her mother will soon appear to reclaim her. Until that day comes, Gilly is determined to make everyone feel as miserable as she does. She is angry, mistrusting and tough—not your typical middle-grade hero. But it is this very stuff, along with rage and determination and an essentially loving nature, that makes Gilly an unforgettable, standout hero.

5) *Create Convincing Motivation.* As I mentioned before, authenticity—of thought, behavior and action—is what makes a character come alive on the page. This concept can be honored in a complex tale about the clash between good and evil or in the simplest book written for little children.

In *The Runaway Bunny*, Margaret Wise Brown's young hero longs to separate from his mother. He also longs to feel safe. Each time the bunny threatens to run away and turn into a fish or a rock or a crocus, his mother assures him that she will find him and take care of him. The bunny's motivation for separating is born out of a child's natural need to grow. The mother's motivation for saving the bunny is her need to protect and reassure her child. Both are motivated by honest emotions and both act honestly on those emotions. The result is a book for the ages.

6) *Reflect Unspoken Feelings in Someone or Something Else.* Often the author explains what a character is thinking or feeling. But this expression of the inner self shouldn't be obvious or overtly stated. Sometimes thoughts can be conveyed in subtle ways, as in the feelings of one character finding a reflection in another.

In *One-Eyed Cat*, Paula Fox's hero, Ned, has been forbidden to touch the rifle in the attic. But one day he gives into temptation, takes the rifle and shoots at a night-evoked shadow. The boy's guilt about taking the rifle stains his conscience. His inner torment escalates to the point of poisoning his life when he sees a cat with a missing eye and assumes this is "the shadow" he shot that fateful night. Fox conveys Ned's anguish in a muted but effective way.

> As he watched the gray cat circle and leap and pounce, he felt light and hopeful; he felt free of an oppressive weight. Then he saw the emptiness of the cat's left eye which the lid half revealed. He saw the way the cat still shook his head from time to time as though something had crawled inside his ear.

Fox doesn't talk about how guilty Ned feels. She shows us, instead, how the cat looks and feels, leaving us to imagine the boy's reaction to the cat's suffering. Reflecting a character's feelings in another being is a quiet and powerful way to convey the inner reality of that character.

7) *Present Multifaceted Villains.* When most people think of a villain, they think of a thoroughly bad guy. But a singularly dark and nefarious character isn't half as interesting as a conflicted villain. As I said before, people are not consistent. An all-bad-all-the-time villain is a boring villain.

In Robert Cormier's groundbreaking book *The Chocolate War,* protagonist Jerry Renault defies school tradition when he refuses to sell chocolates for a school fund-raiser. Through the machinations of a teacher named Brother Leon, gang member Archie Costello is put in charge of disciplining Jerry for his defiance. In the beginning, Archie is painted in one shade of black. Then we learn that Brother Leon is manipulating Archie, just as Archie is manipulating Jerry. This casts a different light on the cruelty of Archie, not so much asking for sympathy as asking for a small measure of understanding of why he is who he is.

8) *Dramatize Feelings.* Writers often tell readers how a character feels instead of showing them. This is a weak and ineffective way to convey a character's inner life.

In *Monster Night at Grandma's House,* Richard Peck tells the story of a boy named Toby who is forced to confront an array of demons who torment him in the darkness of his room. Toby's responses are shown to the reader in a variety of ways.

> He just lay there waiting, the scrap quilt pulled right up to his shut-tight eyes. . . . All at once Toby found it hard to breathe . . .
> He tried to take short quick breaths so that the quilt wouldn't move and give him away.

All these things convey Toby's fear without ever telling the reader he's scared. Whether it's joy, anxiety or sadness, find interesting ways to show the reader what the hero feels. You'll be rewarded with a more intriguing portrait for your efforts and a more enthusiastic audience for your book.

9) *Create Empathetic Situations.* The easiest way to enlist a reader's empathy is to create situations the reader can relate to. Embarrassment, loneliness, longing, fear, happiness, relief, insecurity, anticipation, anxiety—all are universal expressions of the human condition. These feelings tap into the deepest part of a reader's psyche, inviting her to join the hero in sharing the emotions common to us all.

In his remarkable YA novel *A Separate Peace,* John Knowles explores the complexities associated with the demands of friendship, the intrusion of evil and the limits of loyalty at a boys' boarding school. Phineas is the golden boy, the handsome, dazzling athlete all the other students envy. "He possessed an extra vigor, a heightened confidence in himself, a serene capacity for affection which saved him."

Gene is the narrator of the story who looks back on a fateful summer he spent as an insecure, lonely, introverted teen. The novel explores the complex feelings associated with the bond of friendship and the cruelty of adolescents, the corrosion of envy and indifference of evil. And he accomplishes this in a way that invites the reader to experience the emotions—not just read about them—that are presented in the story. It's no wonder this book has been in print for over forty years.

10) *Make Certain the Hero Saves Himself.* Let's say you read a story about an adolescent hero who struggles to escape the tyranny of his father. At the end of the book, when it appears as if the boy will never be able to stand up to this bully, the hero's best friend steps in and calls the authorities, the social worker comes and saves the boy to struggle another day. A happy ending? Yes. But how has the boy grown? He hasn't. What has the boy learned? Nothing. Where is the gratification for the reader? Vanished.

This kind of nonconfrontational ending might work if the boy finds the courage to ask for help and to confront the embarrassment of having been unable to defend himself in the past. However, when it comes to fiction, I am an advocate of a more direct approach.

This is art, not life. The fact is, as well-intentioned or realistic as this solution might be, genuine story-telling satisfaction won't occur unless our young hero learns to defend himself and confront his step-father. Furthermore, this scene must be dramatized "onstage" for the reader, not presented as one character telling another about the confrontation.

Take our intrepid hero Max, for instance. Instead of taming the monsters with his own magic trick, let's say Max meets a friendly wild thing who persuades his fellow wild things to stop picking on the boy. After all, Max is just a scared little kid who's a long way from home. In this scenario, the hero is saved by his wild thing friend, but the story falls flat. Which is why Maurice Sendak has Max save himself. And which leads to my final thought on this subject: *The hero must be the instrument of his own salvation.*

All of these tips are essential to what and how you write about the characters who inhabit your books—multidimensional characters that are layered and complex and intriguing. Each approach can illuminate an aspect of your fictional character and guide you on your way to creating personalities that live on the page as well as in the lasting imaginations of children.

Your Turn
Exercises in Character

1) Read the following books.

- *Olivia*, by Ian Falconer
- *Silent to the Bone*, by E.L. Konigsburg
- *Holes*, by Louis Sachar

Pay special attention to the main characters and how they are presented to the reader. Then ask yourself the following questions.

- What does the main character want the most?
- What must the character overcome?
- What makes the character memorable?
- What does the character learn?
- How is the character's inner life revealed?
- How does the hero save himself?

2) Once you have considered these books and analyzed why the main characters are so successful, make a checklist for your own book. Create a family and geographical background for your hero, beginning with her grandparents. Write down every trait, attribute, fault and peculiarity that applies to your character, and then create an in-depth psychological profile to go along with her.

Finally, ask yourself the following questions.

- Is the hero authentic?
- Is the hero complex?
- Is the hero conflicted?
- Is the hero convincing?
- Is the hero memorable?
- Is the hero emotionally honest?
- Is the hero's motivation justifiable?
- Is the hero the instrument of her own salvation?

If you can answer yes to all these questions, chances are you have created a memorable and lasting character.

CHAPTER FOURTEEN

Point of View

Point of View: "The attitude or outlook of a narrator
or character in a piece of literature."

—The American Heritage Dictionary

POINTS OF VIEW

Point of view creates confusion because the layman's definition—an opinion, a feeling, an attitude—isn't broad enough to include the writer's definition. The latter certainly embraces opinions, feelings and attitudes. But it also encompasses critical choices about who tells the story and how that story is revealed.

In other words, point of view has two parts: the perspective of a story or character, and the way in which that story or character is expressed.

That sounds simple enough. But if you take a closer look, it soon becomes apparent that you're staring into the slippery center of a big can of literary worms.

Point of view is a complex concept that resists simple explanation. For instance, what one person calls "neutral omniscient" another person calls the "objective point of view." Then you have author intrusion vs. subjective viewpoint; point of view character vs. focus character; unreliable narrator vs. authoritative narrator vs. implied narrator; shifting point of view vs. peripheral point of view vs. panoramic point of view.

Enough already. My personal point of view is that this subject has been unnecessarily complicated by too much critical theory and too little common sense. My goal here is to reaffirm the basics.

FIRST THINGS FIRST

Before you start writing your story, it's important to clarify in your own mind the difference between single and multiple viewpoints.

A tale told from a *single point of view* is when you tell the story from one person's perspective only. Everything is filtered through that specific person's eyes, heart and mind. No other character's thoughts or feelings are directly expressed in the book. This does not mean, however, that you can't show how others feel through their actions and reactions to people, places and events.

In a book with *multiple points of view*, the story is told through the eyes, hearts and minds of two or more characters. There are times when a narrative demands such a treatment in order to convey the fullness of the story. You can create the multiple points of view in first or third person. The choice is up to you.

When you're writing for children, it's usually best to maintain a unity of viewpoint. Younger children, especially, become confused if you change points of view in the middle of a story. Once you settle on your point of view, stick to it.

With older kids this unity isn't so relevant. If preteens and adolescents can watch TV, listen to music, talk on the phone and do homework at the same time, they can handle multiple points of view. Piece of cake.

THE DYNAMIC DUO

To determine the point of view of your story, you must ask yourself two critical questions: Who tells the story and how is it told?

Who Do I Want to Tell the Story?

Lots of different people can tell the same story. Each time the narrator changes, the story changes. The writer's task is to choose the most effective character or characters to tell the tale.

Suppose you're writing a book about Matt almost drowning when he was fourteen years old. Do you tell the story from his point of view, his friend's point of view or other people's points of view?

Each of the three approaches would spring from the same set of circumstances, but each would constitute a radically different tale.

· *Matt's point of view.* Here, you could tell the story of how Matt trips and falls off the dock into the water—how helplessness gives way to the monster of panic and how terror surrenders to the bliss of departing.

This approach might be interesting if you want to tell a coming-of-age story. You would focus on Matt's emotions, how a fifteen-minute episode transforms his life forever—what he feels at the time, how the experience changes the way he sees himself and the way he relates to other people.

· *Friend's point of view.* It might be intriguing to read about the experience from Matt's friend's point of view—the kid who pulls Matt out of the water and gives him CPR until the paramedics arrive, the kid who learns what it's like to come close to losing his best friend and how saving his friend's life changes his own life.

If what you want to do is tell a more exciting, action-packed story, this would be the approach. The tension rises out of calling 911, in taking instructions from the operator about how to perform CPR, not knowing if the paramedics are going to arrive in time, or if Matt is going to live or die.

· *Multiple characters' point of view.* To further complicate the issue, you could tell the story about the near-drowning from multiple points of view. Matt can tell the story from his point of view, the friend can tell the story from another point of view, Matt's brother can tell the story from his sibling-rivalry point of view and Matt's mother can tell the story from her maternal point of view.

This approach would be more appropriate if you want to tell a human interest story about how one powerful incident changes each person in a different way. The irony here could be that Matt—the person whose life was in jeopardy—is least affected by the incident.

As you can see, although each story is centered around the same singular incident, each story is entirely different from the other. It all depends on the choices you make about who tells the tale.

Once you decide *who* tells the story, you can move on to the question of *how* the story is told.

How Do I Want to Tell the Story?

Do you tell the story in first person (I did this, and I saw that) or third person (she did this, and she saw that)?

In order to determine how you want to tell your story, it's critical to familiarize yourself with the range of choices available, as well as the advantages and disadvantages of each choice.

FIRST PERSON

In a first-person story, the narrator is the "I" of the story. Everything that happens in the book is told from a singular point of view.

In *Are You in the House Alone?* Richard Peck begins his book with:

> From the first warm night of spring until autumn, Steve and I could slip out to the Pastoninis' cottage on the lake, Powdermill Lake. How often? Ten times? Twelve? I don't re- member now. I kept no diary. We left no clues.

That is first person: one point of view, one person telling the story.

Children, especially, like to read books written in the first person. If the voice is strong and the character interesting, kids find it easy to relate to a hero who speaks directly to them. Readers enjoy getting into the head of someone they don't know. It's not that different from writers living in the head of a character in order to tell a more spellbinding story.

Writers new to the craft of storytelling often choose first person be- cause that's how they've written all their lives in letters and journals. In fact, that's the voice I chose to write my first novel; I didn't know any other way to write. A caveat: It may be comfortable to write from a singular and personal point of view, but it's not always easy.

When you write a story in the first person, your ability to shift from place to place and person to person is limited. Everything you write about must be witnessed by the narrator; you can only observe. You cannot assume anyone thinks or feels anything unless it is manifested in some overt way. Every scene is written from the first-person narrator's singular point of view.

Obviously, your plot development options are limited when you can't report on anything that takes place out of sight of the narrator. You also run the risk of sounding repetitive in your writing. There's no doubt about the fact that too many "*Is*" can become tedious.

Granted, Julius Caesar did all right when he said, *Veni, Vidi, Vici:* "I came, I saw, I conquered." Short, pithy and to the point. But that approach to writing would get old if he went on and on describing the Gallic Wars in the first person. "I raped, I pillaged, I plundered. I burned, I looted, I spoiled. I sacked, I snatched, I savaged. I robbed, I ravaged, I wept. I crushed, I cried, I gloried. I raided, I captured, I won." That's a lot of interesting action destroyed by a lot of *Is*.

That said, if you have a story you want to tell and you want to write it in first person, consider the advantages and disadvantages before you settle on your approach.

Advantages of First Person

You Can Create a Sense of Connection. The intimacy of first person sets up a direct connection between reader and writer.

The Reader Experiences the Intensity of a Personal Story. Kids have a sense that the story is being told just to them, as if someone is whispering secrets from the pages of a book.

You Can Create an Intimate Portrait. Readers feel close to the action and the hero. It's easy to slip your imagination into the mind and heart of a first-person narrator.

You Can Create a Variety of Moods. You can create the mood of your choice by using a singular voice. You can write in the voice of a tough kid or the voice of a dreamy romantic. It all depends on the story you want to tell and the feelings you want to convey.

Disadvantages of First Person

Your Story Is Limited to One Point of View. Since your story cannot expand beyond what the narrator thinks, sees and hears, no action can take place out of sight of the first-person narrator.

The narrator can, however, interpret reactions. "Michael looked worried when his mother asked me about the money," or "Dan's voice shook when he told me what happened."

Closeness to Story Can Diminish Perceptions. If the point-of-view character is too close to the action, he might not have the perspective to tell
an interesting story.

Beware of Dangerous Is. Too many "*Is*" can spoil your prose and bore
the reader.

Trick of the Trade

Although first person is limited to what the narrator sees and thinks,
feels and hears, there is a way to move out of sight of the narrator.

If you want to shift to another location, try having the narrator imagine
the scene. Let's go back to Cathy on the ladder. She knows her friends
are in the park waiting for her. But it's a first-person narrative, so we
have no choice but to stay right there on those rungs with her. Right?
Not exactly. We can shift the action away from Cathy and into her imagination with some fictional abracadabra written in the conditional voice.

> As I clung to the sides of the ladder, I glanced at my watch.
> Five minutes after eleven, I thought. I'm already twenty
> minutes late. I can just imagine what my friends are doing
> now.
> Sean's pacing back and forth while Duncan sits on the
> swing—both of them anxious and annoyed.
> My heart sank. I could see and hear it all. Sean would shrug
> in that "whatever" kind of way he has and look at Duncan.
> "If Cathy doesn't get here in five minutes, we're going to
> have to leave," he'd say. "She won't get a chance at winning
> the trip to Hollywood, and we won't have a camera operator
> for the movie."
> "I can do my job and hers, too," Duncan would say.
> Yeah, I thought as I took a step down the ladder. He'll think
> of something, that's for sure. He'll think of something that
> cuts me out of the movie. And cuts me out of Hollywood.

So there you have it: a way to shift outside the view of the first-person
narrator and still stay within the first-person convention.

Although it requires a little verbal sorcery, shifting the scene by slipping into the imagination of the first-person narrator allows you to change the focus to another place or person. At the same time, you can expand the action and create a narrative latitude the strict first person lacks.

So if you want to write in the first person but think it's too limited, try this technique before you reject the possibility. You might find this narrative sleight of hand is all you need to create a well-rounded, single-point-of-view story.

Which First-Person Character Tells the Story?

In 1991 Canadian author Robertson Davies wrote *Fifth Business*, the first book of his Deptford Trilogy. He quotes Tho. Overskou, *Den Danske Skeuplads* (a man and work that seem to have no traceable origin that I can discover) when he describes a particular role for a specific character.

> . . . those roles which, being neither those of Hero nor Hero-
> ine, Confidante nor Villain, but which were nonetheless
> essential to bring about the Recognition or the dénouement,
> were called Fifth Business in drama and opera companies
> organized according to the old style; the player who acted
> these parts was often referred to as Fifth Business.

With this in mind, consider the possibility that when you write your story in first person, the narrator doesn't always have to be the main character. The narrator can be someone whose ordinary, forgettable act has extraordinary ramifications—ramifications that create the conflict around which the story is built. Or the narrator can be removed from the protagonist in a significant way—someone who witnesses the action from a distance, perhaps a brother, a friend or a classmate.

The first way many of us might have encountered this last approach to storytelling is in high school when we read F. Scott Fitzgerald's *The Great Gatsby*. Although the main character of the novel is Jay Gatsby, the story is told by Nick Carraway, an observer rather than a direct partic-ipant in the action. This narrative technique allows the story to be told in a dispassionate voice, since the outsider sometimes sees more, and even knows more, than the people directly involved in the story.

The narrator of *Walk Two Moons*, for example, is a thirteen-year-old girl named Salamanca who tells a story she learned from her friend Phoebe. Author Sharon Creech ends chapter one with the following paragraphs.

> My father started chipping away at a plaster wall in the living room of our house in Bybanks shortly after my mother left us one April morning. . . . Each night as he waited to hear from my mother, he chipped away at that wall.
>
> On the night that we got the bad news—that she was not returning—he pounded and pounded on that wall with a chisel and a hammer. At two o'clock in the morning, he came up to my room. I was not asleep. He led me downstairs and showed me what he had found. Hidden behind the wall was a brick fireplace.
>
> The reason that Phoebe's story reminds me of that plaster wall and the hidden fireplace is that beneath Phoebe's story was another one. Mine.

The novel then continues with Salamanca telling Phoebe's story, but living and revealing her own story at the same time. Each story reflects and deepens the other.

A Survivor's Tale. Patricia Polacco uses a different first-person approach in *Pink and Say*. Based on a true incident in the author's family, this is an extraordinary picture book about two boys—one black and one white—who are captured and dragged to Andersonville prison during the Civil War. The story is narrated by a great-great-great-great-granddaughter of one of the prisoners.

Conceiving of the narrator as the character who has lived to tell the tale has a long and venerable literary tradition. In Herman Melville's *Moby Dick*, Ishmael is the lone survivor of Captain Ahab's mad quest to destroy the great white whale. And it is Ishmael who tells the story of the ill-fated crew of the *Pequod*. In the Book of Job, one after the other, four messengers bring increasingly horrific news to the tragic hero. Each man ends his story with, "and I only am escaped alone to tell thee."

Rethinking First Person. The survivor's tale is just one way to approach first person. If you want to write in the first person and you're stuck in the narrative, consider the possibility that the wrong person is telling the story.

Just as in life, sometimes a person can render a more intriguing response to an incident that he witnesses from afar, an incident he learns about rather than experiences. Choosing a narrator distanced from the story can give you more leeway to comment on the action of the characters and evaluate their responses to each other. And it can also give you a more surprising perspective on the events that take place.

So before you lock yourself in to the protagonist telling your first-person story, think about how your story might unfold if it were told from the point of view of another character, even a minor one. A singular advantage of using an observer-narrator is that the reader learns about the action at the same time the narrator does. Nothing is revealed before its time, an approach that might allow you to tell the story in a more interesting and compelling way.

First-Person Moods

The first-person narration works at all age levels. Early chapter book readers enjoy it just as much as teenagers. One of the pleasures of writing in first person is that you can create such a variety of moods. Serious and funny, casual and formal, angry and gentle. It's all there for you to explore.

In *Junie B. Jones and a Little Monkey Business*, Barbara Park writes her chapter book in a casual, amusing style. She uses first person to draw the reader into the story.

> My name is Junie B. Jones. The B stands for Beatrice. Except
> I don't like Beatrice. I just like B and that's all.

Eve Bunting creates a totally different first-person mood in her middle-grade detective story *Coffin on a Case*. There's more intensity here, more of a sense of immediacy that pulls the reader along. The action moves at a fast clip and the short sentences reflect this.

She was beside me before I could get my mind to accept
what I had seen. She grabbed my arm and dragged me up
the steps. One hand covered my mouth. I could see her face,
grim, angry, not smiling anymore. Man, was she strong.
Strong as a sumo wrestler. I tried to break away, to kick at
her shins. I tried to bite but I couldn't. She yanked me
inside the house, slammed the door and threw me across the
room the same way someone would throw a Frisbee.

In *The House on Mango Street,* Sandra Cisneros ends her evocative
novel with words that invite both elegy and wonder. You don't need to
read this book for the narrator to come alive in the reader's mind.

One day I will pack my bags of books and paper. One day I
will say goodbye to Mango. I am too strong for her to keep
me here forever. One day I will go away.
　　Friends and neighbors will say, What happened to that
Esperanza? Where did she go with all those books and paper? Why did she march so far away?
　　They will not know I have gone away to come back. For the
ones I left behind. For the ones who cannot out.

Three first-person books, three different moods. The possibilities
are endless. The decision you must make is how to balance the advantages and disadvantages of first person in order to tell the best possible story.

First-Person Books to Check Out.

- *The Watsons Go to Birmingham—1963* by Christopher Paul Curtis

- *Dancing on the Edge* by Han Nolan

- *Don't Call Me Beanhead!* by Susan Wojciechowski

- *A Fine White Dust* by Cynthia Rylant

- *Snazzy Aunties* by Nick Sharratt

THIRD PERSON, SINGLE POINT OF VIEW

In the third person, single point of view, you tell the story using "he said, she said" dialogue tags. But you still confine the action to one person's thoughts, feelings and point of view.

In a way, this is an expanded version of the first-person narration. The "I" becomes a "he" or a "she." You still can't get in anyone else's head or witness any action outside the knowledge of this particular character. You stay with a single, designated character, telling the story exclusively from his single, designated viewpoint.

If this is the case, you might be tempted to ask why you should bother leaving the first-person narrative at all. It's so cozy there, so familiar. You've already got a handle on that approach.

Advantages of Third Person, Single Point of View

The Reader Identifies With a Specific Character. As in first person, this technique enlists the allegiance of the reader and invites a strong emotional identification with one specific character.

Your Narrative Horizons are Expanded. This shift in perspective is not as limiting as you might imagine, nor as restrictive as some people would have you believe. Here, you can devise one voice for the protagonist and a different one for the narrator, giving you the latitude to play voice and tone against each other.

For instance, if the narrator of the story is an angry kid, but the tone of the book—the story being told—is magical and elegiac, the interplay between these different moods can create an intriguing and memorable story.

Here, as in first person, you can create a narrative shift to another location by having the character imagine a distant scenario.

Your Ability to Offer Emotional Insights Is Deepened. Some people believe telling your story from this point of view diminishes your ability to evoke the feelings, thoughts and passions of the hero. Not so. It's just as easy to get into the head of a character in third-person narration as it is in first person.

Your Opportunity to Interpret Events Is Enlarged. The narrator, as well as the viewpoint character, can comment on events, allowing the author greater latitude in opening doors to understanding.

Disadvantages of Third Person, Single Point of View

Your Viewpoint Is Limited to One Character. Just as in first person, you can still only tell your story through one character's eyes.

It's Harder to Balance the Narration. It's a greater challenge to balance the author's voice with the third person, single voice that's viewing the events.

Stacked against the advantages of this point of view, however, I don't view these drawbacks as inhibiting.

Debunking the Myth

There are writers who claim that when you shift out of the first person point of view you lose the intimacy and connection with the reader. Nothing could be further from the truth. You can still get into a character's head and heart, and you can still mine the depth of the feelings the character experiences. To accomplish this you must remain more conscious of showing (not telling) how the character feels.

Let's look at *The Great Gilly Hopkins.* Katherine Paterson tells her story totally from Gilly's point of view, but she loses no opportunity to invite the reader to feel what Gilly feels and to experience what she experiences. When Gilly, a foster child shunted from home to home, becomes convinced she must leave her current residence, Paterson writes:

> All at once, leaving Thompson Park became urgent. Gilly
> knew in the marrow of her bones that if she stayed much
> longer, this place would mess her up. Between the craziness
> in the brown house and the craziness at school, she would
> become like W.E., soft and no good, and if there was anything
> her short life had taught her, it was that a person must be
> tough. Otherwise you were had.

Paterson conveys all the pain of Gilly's feelings, yet she also comments on the hero's situation from a deeper perspective. No passion is lost, no insight is sacrificed. On the one hand, we feel the anguish of this young woman caught in the system. On the other, we begin to understand the complexity of her trap.

A perspective frequently used in children's literature, the third person, single point of view is an intriguing way to tell a story, especially if you want to focus on the events in the life of one character. Depending on the voice of the author and the mood of the protagonist, you can create the same variety of feelings that you can in first person, evoking either complementary or contradictory moods as you do it.

Third Person, Single Point of View Books to Check Out.
- *No Tooth, No Quarter!* by John Buller and Susan Schade
- *The Burning Questions of Bingo Brown* by Betsy Cromer Byars
- *Everyone Else's Parents Said Yes* by Paula Danziger
- *The Great Gilly Hopkins* by Katherine Paterson
- *Snuffles Makes a Friend* by Mary Lee Donovan

THIRD PERSON, LIMITED POINT OF VIEW

In third person, limited point of view, the author tells the story in the third person (he said, she said) but from more than one point of view. If you want to focus on two or three characters, this is the narrative approach you would choose.

Again, don't be misled into thinking you must sacrifice the intimacy of feelings and the connection with reader when you use this voice. It does, however, require more effort to explore hidden places and maintain the bond between the character and reader. But you can achieve this by entering the character's thoughts and showing his actions and reactions to a variety of circumstances.

In children's books, this technique would not be used in first books or early chapter books. Younger kids need to concentrate on a focused point of view when they're first learning to read. Older readers can easily handle this technique.

Advantages of Third Person, Limited Point of View

You Can Convey a Fuller Story. Instead of telling the story from just one point of view, this method allows you to expand your horizons and witness other events without losing the tight focus on two or three main characters.

You Can Get Into the Head of More Than One Character. Instead of being limited to the thoughts and feelings of one single character, you can deepen the insight into the emotional state of several characters, thereby deepening the reader's appreciation of the events and dilemmas you present.

You Have a Better Chance for Reader Identification. This approach offers the opportunity to create a strong identification between the reader and more than one character.

If you have several characters who play central roles in the plot, the reader can experience the thoughts and feelings of all these characters. This increases the understanding of the conflicts and allows the writer to state the case for more than one person's point of view.

You Can Create a Conflict in the Reader's Mind. If you paint full portraits of two or three characters, you can then set up questions for the reader to consider. Who is right in this situation? Which path would I choose? How would I behave here? Even though I identify with this character, I can understand that one. Feelings such as this keep the reader interested in the story since he wants to know how the conflict will be resolved and which character will be proven right.

It's Easier to Paint the World in Shades of Gray. By the time they reach the third or fourth grade, most kids are beginning to suspect they don't live in a black and white world.

Younger children expect a world with strong distinctions between good and bad. Older children understand that this is not the way the world works. They also appreciate the opportunity to read stories in which life is portrayed in a more complex and realistic fashion.

Disadvantages of Third Person, Limited Point of View

You Can Lose Your Pinpoint Focus on One Character. Once you spread the point of view to other characters, you run the risk of diluting the reader's identification with the character. However, I don't consider this much of a disadvantage, since careful writing can prevent this from happening.

You Must Pay Special Attention to Delineating Your Voices. If you switch between several points of view, it's critical to be clear about who is speaking in each scene and who is witnessing each event. The reader should never have to pause and figure out whose point of view is being expressed.

In *The Summer of the Swans*, Betsy Byars takes advantage of the third

person, limited point of view. Here, the author shifts between Sara Godfrey and her mentally retarded brother Charlie. Most of the focus in the
middle-grade novel stays with Sara. But in order to convey the full measure of fear Charlie experiences when he gets lost in the woods, Byars
changes to his point of view, allowing the reader to identify with the
helplessness and terror that wash over Charlie as he huddles alone in
the forest ravine.

In the first chapter, Sara Godfrey tells her brother:

> "Charlie, I'll tell you something. This has been the worst
> summer of my life."
> She did not know exactly why this was true. . . . It was as if
> her life was a huge kaleidoscope, and the kaleidoscope had
> been turned and now everything was changed. The same
> stones, shaken, no longer made the same design.

In the second chapter, Charlie breaks his sucker and his sister tries to
help him.

> He began to shake his head slowly from side to side. His
> eyes were squeezed shut.
> "I'm not going to take it away from you. I'm going to fix it
> one more time."
> He was unwilling to trust her and continued to shake his
> head.

Here, different incidents are told from two different points of view.
We're able to empathize with each character's feelings as we move
through the story.

In *The Great Mom Swap* by Betsy Haynes, a story about two best friends
and next-door neighbors who exchange mothers, the point of view shifts
between the two girls throughout the novel. In order to tell the story in
the fullest way, it's important for the reader to understand how each
girl feels as she lives her temporarily new and improved life.

Both Byars and Haynes give their readers the opportunity to identify fully with more than one character. This is, after all, the goal of telling a story from this point of view.

Third Person, Limited Point of View Books to Check Out.

• *A Bone From a Dry Sea* by Peter Dickinson

• *Bat 6* by Virginia Euwer Wolff

• *P.S. Longer Letter Later* by Paula Danziger and Ann M. Martin

• *Ernestine & Amanda* by Sandra Belton

THIRD PERSON, OMNISCIENT POINT OF VIEW

Omniscient point of view means that the author knows everything. Stories told from an omniscient point of view offer multiple ways of looking at a given incident. If five people witness one incident, the author can express how each is feeling at that moment. The author assumes a god-like position, looking down from the mountain and narrating what he sees below.

The omniscient point of view isn't used as frequently as the other approaches to storytelling. In spite of the fact this technique allows the author the greatest range, it is fraught with pitfalls. Unless this approach is executed with consummate skill, the omniscient viewpoint can weaken a story and dilute the reader's allegiance to any single character. Furthermore, the omniscient voice can be confusing to young readers.

That said, if your goal is to get into the head of lots of characters, this is the point of view for you. Your story is not limited to the world as witnessed through the eyes of one or two characters. The viewpoint is sweeping, and the narrator's voice is often stronger than the individual characters. Here, the narrator plays God.

A.A. Milne's *Winnie-the-Pooh*, one of the great classics of children's literature, uses the omniscient point of view. The author shifts from character to character, touching each one lightly as he tells his story. The voice A.A. Milne adopts has a detached amusement about it that dominates the storytelling. Even when the author talks about Pooh being scared or anxious, he doesn't try to get into Pooh's head beyond conveying the gentle anxiety the bear feels.

Furthermore, although the narrator addresses Christopher Robin directly, he doesn't stay exclusively in his head. Christopher asks questions, and they are answered. He interacts with the characters in the book, but we aren't invited to share only his thoughts and feelings; all of the characters come into play. One minute we're reading the story from Christopher's point of view, the next minute we're reading from Pooh's.

In fact, often the point of view changes in the same paragraph.

> So they [Pooh and Piglet] went on, feeling just a little anx-
> ious now, in case the three animals in front of them were
> of Hostile Intent. And Piglet wished very much that his
> grandfather T.W. were there, instead of elsewhere, and
> Pooh thought how nice it would be if they met Christopher
> Robin suddenly but quite accidentally, and only because he
> liked Christopher Robin so much. And then, all of a sudden,
> Winnie-the-Pooh stopped again, and licked the tip of his
> nose in a cooling manner, for he was feeling more hot and
> anxious than ever in this life before.

At the opposite end of the literary spectrum, in *Maniac Magee*—another book with an omniscient point of view—Jerry Spinelli also uses the narrator's voice as a powerful character in its own right.

> As for the first person to actually stop and talk with Maniac,
> that would be Amanda Beale. And it happened because of
> a mistake.
> It was around eight in the morning, and Amanda was head-
> ing for grade school, like hundreds of other kids all over
> town. What made Amanda different was that she was carrying
> a suitcase, and that's what caught Maniac's eye. He figured
> she was like him, running away, so he stopped and said "Hi."
> Amanda was suspicious.

In both of these passages, the author's narrative voice becomes a character in its own right. Both voices are tailored to the tale, supporting the fact that the omniscient point of view is intriguing to use. But it is also challenging and requires great skill.

Advantages of the Omniscient Point of View

You Can Get Into Lots of Characters' Heads. You can present your story from many viewpoints and convey the private thoughts and feelings of multiple characters.

You Can Tell Your Story From a Broader Perspective. Since you're not limited to what one or two characters experience, you have a wider scope in how to present your story.

You Can Play One Character's Feelings Against Another. If three kids witness the same scene, you can show why each feels the way he does and how their ideas conflict with one another.

Disadvantages of the Omniscient Point of View

You Risk Diluting the Reader's Identification With Any Singular Character. When too many stories are being told, the reader loses interest in any one character.

It's Too Easy for the Reader to Become Confused About Who Feels What. Too many individual stories opens the reader up to too many points of view and opinions.

You Can Lose the Inherent Passion of a Story That is Limited to One or Two Points of View. If everyone has strong feelings about a given incident, all the feelings can be diluted.

It's Easy for the Reader to Lose Focus on the Heart of the Story. If there are too many stories to tell, one story has a hard time dominating the action and capturing the reader.

Nine Tips for Using the Omniscient Point of View

1) Choose Dominating Characters. When you tell the story from multiple points of view, you can maintain reader allegiance by having one or two characters dominate the action.

2) Emphasize Main Characters. When using multiple characters, don't spread your story so evenly that you deprive the reader of identifying with one or two main characters.

3) Beware of Detachment. Beware of a voice that is so removed from the action you lose the reader's ability to identify with the characters.

4) Create Deliberate Shifts. Make the shifts from character to character early on in the story so the reader comes to expect these changes.

5) Stick With Your Point of View. With rare exceptions—*Winnie-the-Pooh* being a major one—do not change your point of view in the middle of a scene.

6) Parcel Out Information. Beware of divulging too much information and diluting the suspense in the story.

7) Keep Your Characters in Check. Just because you can have your characters go anywhere and do anything, that doesn't mean you should. If they stray from the essentials of the story, you dilute the focus and lose your reader.

8) Control Gratuitous Shifts to Other Points of View. If the viewpoint of a character doesn't make a significant contribution to the scene or the story, don't use it.

9) Avoid the Trap of a Mandatory Revelation. Shifting the point of view to another character can force you to reveal information you don't want disclosed—information that would spoil the surprise. For instance, if the character knows a secret about something he has witnessed, you can't withhold this information if you shift into his thoughts and feelings.

Third Person, Omniscient Point of View Books to Check Out.

• *The Hitchhiker's Guide to the Galaxy* by Douglas Adams

• *Killing Mr. Griffin* by Lois Duncan

• *Julie of the Wolves* by Jean Craighead George

• *The Chocolate War* by Robert Cormier

• *The Complete Tales of Winnie-the-Pooh* by A.A. Milne

Multiple Points of View: Who's Speaking Now?

If you choose to tell your story from multiple points of view—from more than one character's eyes and heart and mind—make it clear who is speaking, thinking and feeling at any given moment. For the beginning writer, especially, it helps to have a strong idea of how you are going to distinguish your voices.

If you decide to use two or more viewpoint characters, it's a good idea to find a way to distinguish or differentiate them so there's no mistaking which viewpoint character is telling the story at any given moment.

Thirteen Ways to Distinguish Multiple Points of View Using Third Person, Omniscient

1) Separate the Points of View. When you shift from one viewpoint character to the other, create a break with a double-space or other marker to indicate change.

2) Change the Point of View When You Change Your Scene. Narrate separate scenes from separate points of view.

3) Create Parallel Responses. Write a story in which the hero behaves one way in "real" life and then secretly responds in a totally different way in her journal or diary.

4) Try the Epistolary Approach. Tell the whole story through the exchange of letters, postcards or e-mail between multiple characters.

5) Write One Voice in Italic and the Other in Nonitalic. Think of this approach as a duet, with one character telling about an incident from one point of view and another character offering a different point of view. Differentiate them with typeface.

6) Set Up a Pattern of Change. Alternate chapters or scenes so the reader comes to expect the shift from one character to the other. This technique not only offers clarity, it creates a sense of anticipation in the reader about what the other character will think or say or do next.

• *Note:* If you set up a regular pattern, consider a way to vary the pattern occasionally so the reader doesn't become bored with the predictability.

7) Take Advantage of Timelines. If you have three or four characters telling the story, break the book up into clearly delineated chronological timelines in which you tell the story of one specific character.

For instance, you could do this with days or months. *September: Lisa and Serge. November: Joe and Serge. May: Lisa, Joe and Serge.* Each person has a chapter or a section in September and November and May. In the last section, all their stories come together.

8) Take Advantage of Locations. For instance, you would head your chapters *Mark Twain Middle School: Sue Lin. Heather. Sheila. Fashion Arena Shopping Center: Sue Lin. Sheila. MacArthur Park: Sheila. Heather.*

9) Alternate Chapters. If your events are happening simultaneously and

Warning!

As I said before, avoid switching points of view in the same paragraph or in the same scene. Generally speaking, your story will be stronger if you play each scene from one viewpoint only.

A Warning About That Warning!
Now that I've made this big blanket statement, allow me to remind you of something we've been told since we first started reading children's books: There's an exception to every rule. You saw it in *Winnie-the-Pooh*, and you can see it in *The Facts and Fictions of Minna Pratt*. In this middle-grade novel, Patricia MacLachlan breaks the rules about limiting the point of view of one character per scene. As T.S. Eliot said, "It's not wise to violate the rules until you know how to observe them." And certainly, MacLachlan knows how to observe all the conventions.

In the space of two paragraphs, the author shifts skillfully from the point of view of one character to another. The reader is never in doubt about who is thinking what. But she's also never in doubt that the story belongs to Minna Pratt, the main character.

> Minna smiles at her brother. He is small and stocky and compact like a suitcase. Minna loves him. McGrew always tells the truth, even when he shouldn't. He is kind. And he lends Minna money from the coffee jar he keeps beneath his mattress.
> . . . But this is only one life. A different one. A better one. McGrew knows this, too. McGrew is ten years old. He knows nearly everything. He knows, for instance, that his older sister, Minna Pratt, age eleven, is sitting patiently next to her cello waiting to be a woman.

In spite of Patricia MacLachlan's skillful insurrection, I would strongly suggest that beginners stick with the rules until they have the narrative experience to break them.

two characters are telling about them, alternate chapters between the two points of view.

Clarify the fact that the actions are happening alongside each other by noting the time, day, date or some other significant event. The last chapter should resolve everything.

10) Split the Pages. Place Jack's commentary on the left and Annie's on the right.

11) Have the Voices Alternate Chapters. If you're telling the story in a sequential fashion, have Mohammed narrate the first chapter, Gabriella the second and Jenny the third.

12) Change the Location of the Action. When you do this, the second voice takes over the story when the location changes. You shift to a new locale, you shift to a new point of view. Meanwhile, back at the ranch . . .

13) Alternate Emphasis. Give the voice of your main character greater emphasis, with the secondary character(s) commenting at the beginning or end of each chapter.

POINT OF VIEW ADDENDUM: SECOND PERSON

Every once in a while a book is written in second person singular—i.e., "you do this" and "you see that." This narrative approach is used for a specific reason, such as creating a story in which the reader becomes the main character.

As a matter of fact, all my Which Way and Secret Door books were written in the second person. These are the branching-book adventures designed to pull the reader directly into the action in order to make choices about what happens next.

For instance, *Giants, Elves and Scary Monsters*, a Secret Door book for younger kids, begins with:

It is dark outside. You have gone to bed, but you are still wide awake.

You lie quietly until everyone in the house is asleep. Then you creep out of bed and tiptoe into the closet.

You push away the clothes and knock three times on the back wall. Soon the secret door begins to move. It opens just wide enough for you to slip through.

You step into a strange land.
A band of giants is marching toward you from one direction.
A band of elves is coming from the other side . . .
If you go with the elves, turn to page 4.
If you go with the giants, turn to page 6.

You get the idea. The reader, herself, becomes the hero of the story and the center of the action. In rare cases, and in specific genres, this approach can be effective. But generally speaking, a second-person narration is an unorthodox, gimmicky and ineffective way to tell a tale.

So there you have it: Point of view encompasses the two critical questions of *who* tells the story and *how* that story is told. The choices you make will have a radical effect on the story you tell. Don't be afraid to experiment with different approaches. The goal isn't to be right the first time you try; the goal is to be effective and memorable the last time you try.

Your Turn

Finding Your Focus

1) Read one book from each of the categories listed in this chapter: first person; third person, limited; third person, omniscient.
  As you read each book, ask yourself the following questions.

- If the story is told from more than one point of view, how does the author distinguish the different voices?
- How does the author shift points of view?
- Why do you think the author chose to tell the story from this point of view?
- How would the story change if it were told from a single point of view? From multiple points of view?
- How does the author use the point of view to increase suspense?

- Do you think the author chose the strongest point of view to tell this story?

2) Once you've considered these questions carefully, rewrite the opening pages of each book from two new points of view.

- What advantages and disadvantages did you find in each approach?
- What information do you have to include or delete in order to shift points of view?

3) Before you settle on the point of view from which to write your own story, ask yourself the following questions.

- What are the advantages and disadvantages of the different narrative voices?
- What mood am I trying to convey? Formal? Informal? Casual? Ominous? Playful?
- Do I want the narrator's voice to act as another character or to fade into the background?
- Which character or characters would tell the story in the most interesting way?

CHAPTER FIFTEEN

Inner and Outer Dialogue

Dialogue is a very useful tool to reveal things about people, and novels are about people and what they do to each other.

—*Thomas McGuane*

DIALOGUE

I have a friend whose father is a noted screenwriter. He tells me that when he was growing up, he and his brother would be sitting in the back seat of the car as their father drove them to the beach, and suddenly their dad would utter some total non sequitur. Then, while carrying on an ostensible conversation with his sons, he would enter into an extended, mumbled discourse with unseen people, working out dialogue between characters for one movie scene after another as he drove.

I have a hunch that lots of writers "hear" thoughts and dialogue as they go through their days. You don't have to be working on a specific scene or project to do this. You just have to listen to the thoughts that cross your mind in a constant stream throughout your conscious hours. If you don't hear them as a matter of course, make an effort to access them. Do yoga, deep breathing or meditation exercises that still your mind. It's in the silence that the voices speak loudest.

In the interest of full disclosure, I should tell you that my capacity for visual imagination is limited. Most of my thoughts come in words, not pictures. I go through my days with a running monologue playing in my head. I not only hear dialogue, I speak it out loud. Lest you suspect I'm a crazy lady given to walking along the beach and chatting with imaginary friends, I hasten to assure you that I used to talk to myself, but I don't anymore. Now I talk to my dog.

A Practical Consideration

On a practical level, when you're writing for children, dialogue opens up a page. There's value in white space. Even for an adult, a page of one or two paragraphs filled with solid print can intimidate a reader. For a child, this sight can discourage reading the book altogether.

As a personal aside, I've not seen any studies on the layout of a page and the willingness to read it. But I suspect lots of readers, both adult and children, recoil at the sight of a solid page of prose. There are hundreds of thousands of books out there that kids can choose from to read. The solid-page-of-print problem is why, when I'm not using dialogue, I try to write in short paragraphs. The visual relief that indents create makes the page more inviting and the reading experience more accessible and enjoyable.

THOUGHTS ON THOUGHT

Dialogue comes in two distinct flavors: inner and outer. Just as speech reveals character, so does thought.

When a character responds to a given situation, her thoughts should reflect who she is. She's not going to change her core self just because she's thinking instead of speaking.

This doesn't, of course, mean that a shy kid only thinks shy thoughts. In fact, his thoughts could reflect the opposite of what he is saying or doing.

Let's say Juan, a shy introvert, is being shoved around by a bigger kid on the playground. Even though he's acquiescing to the bully, Juan could be thinking he-man thoughts such as, I'll tear you limb from limb. I'm gonna beat the daylights out of you.

On the other hand, Maggie might talk tough, but her thoughts would reflect her fear.

"Get away from me, you creep!" Maggie said. She stared at the boy, her voice growling with indignation. Oh God, don't let me start crying now, she thought. Please don't let me cry.

Whether the protagonist's thoughts work in tandem with his actions or run counter to them, whether he has a rich fantasy life or is rooted in reality, make certain his character is revealed by what and how he thinks.

The Mechanics of Thought

It used to be that when a character was thinking, the way you defined this inner process was by saying Jamie thought this, Liz thought that. These days, some writers have turned their backs on that tradition and are putting thoughts in italics. This removes the necessity for the tag line and allows for more creative room to move. Thoughts can be interjected alongside dialogue without stopping to define them as thought.

Warning!

1) Italics are one thing; quotation marks are another. I recently edited a book in which the author insisted on putting thoughts in quotes. There were multiple instances in which I couldn't distinguish between spoken and imagined dialogue. This said, I hope it's clear that you should never put your character's thoughts between quotation marks, especially if you intend to mix them with spoken dialogue.

2) Writers often use thoughts to further the story and explain its subtext. I would caution you, however, to use this tool sparingly. Sometimes you can explain too much, telling instead of showing and depriving the reader of working out some of the subtleties of the story for himself.

THOUGHTS ON DIALOGUE

Contrary to what many writers think, dialogue shouldn't be a replica of speech. Reading a book that reflects how people actually speak can be a drag.

"Like, you know, uhh, like aaa maybe that wouldn't be such umm a
sterling idea."

The goal of writing dialogue is not to mimic how people speak, although mimicking some people might work well. The goal of writing
dialogue is to create the illusion of truth.

When you create dialogue, try to communicate a point without addressing it head-on. For instance, in *The World's Greatest Toe Show*, I wanted
to convey that arch enemy Bunny Bigelow is a prig and the Canal Street
Gang were regular kids. I didn't tell the reader that Bunny was prissy;
I had Bunny criticize the way the gang was decorating their Toe Show
booth at the school fair.

In an effort to provide some privacy for the showing of the toe, the kids
bring sheets from home to hang over the wooden frame of the booth. Then
Bunny gets a look at the multicolored, many-design bedding.

> "Dinosaurs, Mickey Mouse and astronauts?" said Bunny
> Bigelow in her snootiest voice. . . .
> "Our booth is color coordinated. It's decorated in various
> shades of periwinkle and cranberry."
> "It looks like red and blue to me," said Tulu.

It's not hard to figure out what kind of girl Bunny is. Her color-
coordinated attitude conveys her arrogance, just as Tulu's naïve remark
conveys her essential innocence.

Dialogue as Character

Each of your main characters should have a different way of using words.
Just as you and I speak differently, so should your characters.

Rhonda: I don't give a damn about that.

Shannon: Why don't you remind me why I should care?

Ryan: Why should I think this is important?

Carolyn: I'm outta here.

Toni: Caring's not a concept that intrigues me enough to embrace it.

Kevin: Why on *earth* should someone in my position bother with that?

Jenny: Like, I should waste my time with this?

George: Forget it.

Fiona: That's not worth thinking about.

All of these characters are saying the same thing in a different way. Some people ask questions, others make blunt statements. Each of the characters you create should have a distinctive voice. This is what makes dialogue true and what makes fiction compelling.

Six Tricks of the Dialogue Trade

1) Create Dialogue That Reveals Character. There's a difference between "I dunno" and "I haven't the foggiest notion." Your character's speech should reveal who your character is.

2) Create an Authentic Voice for Each Character. In theory, you shouldn't have to identify who's speaking because each character's voice should be distinct. That's not always possible. But it is possible to make certain you believe what the character is saying and how she says it. As you write your dialogue, ask yourself if the words are being true to who the character is. Would a seven-year-old kid from a farm in Nebraska ask, "Wazzup, bro? How's it hanging?" Hardly.

3) Avoid Trendy Slang. Slang can date your book. Today's cool words can be tomorrow's passé lingo. Neat and keen used to be rad. If you have a fantasy about your book staying in print for a long time, don't tie your narrative to dated words or trendy language unless you are trying to plant your story in a specific time and place.

4) Make Certain Your Voices Are Distinct. John doesn't speak like Becky who doesn't speak like Clio. Even when kids try to speak alike, their voices have a different rhythm and different emphasis. "There's no way I'm going to do that" is distinct from "No way am I going to do that."

5) Define Action and Character By Giving the Speaker Something to Do. Rather than putting all the description in the exposition, tag some of it onto dialogue.

"I'm not nervous," Kate said as she glanced at the door.

"What makes you think I'm going to die?" Ron asked, taking another puff of his cigarette.

This kind of "business" can be used to reveal character or give a hint about the action. Although this amplification of action is effective, use it judiciously.

6) Speak As You Write. When I create dialogue, I repeat the words out loud as I write. The difference between how words sound in your head and how they sound coming out of your mouth is the difference between artifice and authenticity.

To tell the truth, I probably repeat 75 percent of what I write out loud. Whether it's dialogue or exposition, it helps my creative process to hear how the words hang together, how the sentences sound before they've received the final blessing of the printed page.

Five Dialogue No-Nos

1) Beware of Repetition. Say it once and say it well. It doesn't take long for dialogue to become boring. As in, "There's not a chance I'm going to do that. Not enough money in the world to make me. Not gonna happen."

2) Avoid Fancy Tag Lines. Keep your tag lines simple. The eye is accustomed to skipping over the "saids" as in "he said" and "she said." On the other hand, "he opined," "she questioned," "she queried," "he inquired" and "she replied" jump off the page and interfere with the narrative. They also alert the editor that the dialogue is written by a novice.

3) Beware of Inaccurate Tag Line Verbs. "Guess again!" he laughed/ grimaced/wept. None of these words describe the actual act of speaking; they describe what the character is doing when he speaks. Try it this way instead: "Guess again," he said with a laugh.

4) Don't Use Proper Names to Distinguish Who's Speaking. Lots of writers new to the game think they can avoid defining who's speaking by using proper names in the dialogue. As in:

"Well, Joyce, I think it's your dog that's causing the problem."

"Why would you say that, Chris?"

Unless they are trying to make a specific point, people rarely use proper names in dialogue. This is not a clever way to avoid using "he said/she said." It's another way to identify yourself as a novice.

5) Don't Disguise Preaching By Slipping It Into Dialogue. In our urge to moralize, sometimes we think we can sneak a message into the dialogue and nobody will know the difference.

Wrong.

> "I don't know why he smokes so much pot."
> "Doesn't he know that marijuana is addictive?"
> "I just read a study that says smoking pot changes your chromosomes."

"Not to mention the fact that heavy use impairs your memory."

The reader's response to this preachy dialogue? Rolled eyes, disdain and the permanently closed covers of a book. If you want to convey this message in your story, the best advice is to write a story whose characters and actions demonstrate the antidrug message.

Your Turn

Speak Easys

1) Convert the following scenario into dialogue spoken by the following characters. Use different dialogue for each set of characters.

Scenario: Jack and Jill go up a hill to fetch a pail of water. Jack falls down and breaks his crown, and Jill comes tumbling after.

Characters:

• Jack and Jill as a couple married for fifty years.

• Jack and Jill in nursery school.

• Jack and Jill at a rave.

• Jack and Jill in high school.

• Jack and Jill as bickering siblings.

2) Take the first major set of dialogue in your book, and write it in three different ways. After you write each set, ask yourself the following questions.

• Does this dialogue feel authentic?

• Have I struck the right mood?

• Have I conveyed what I want to say in the best way possible?

• Is there anything I can do to tighten the dialogue?

• Do I believe what the characters are saying?

PART FOUR

Interior
Designs

CHAPTER SIXTEEN

Promise, Premise, Theme and Moral

No one can write decently who is distrustful of the reader's intelligence, or whose attitude is patronizing.

—*E.B. White*

THE PROMISE

When we talked about endings, we talked about the importance of keeping your fictional promise. What you say and how you say it sets up specific expectations. When you write the opening to your book, never forget you are offering a contract to your reader. You are making a promise.

Inherent in this promise is your willingness to remove yourself from the story in order to let a character's action speak for itself. The intrusion of the author's voice and opinions on those of the character interrupts the reader's experience and dilutes the believability of the story.

Also inherent in the promise you make is the fact that when you create a contract with your reader, you are bound to honor it. You can't sort of keep your promise; there's no wiggle room here. You can't start out with a thriller introduction and move into a cozy sibling drama. The reader depends on you to stick to your fictional guns.

Even though the promise colors the background of your book, all the aspects that make up this agreement need to be examined before you write your story. You make your promise in four basic ways:

- With your premise
- With your theme
- With your voice
- With your tone

We'll examine premise and theme in this chapter and save voice and tone for the next chapter.

Bait and Switch

Lest you be tempted to lure the reader into a story with a light, amusing beginning and then shift to a different story, there is a price to pay for breaking your promise. Years ago my fifth-grade son read a book by a well-known, award-winning author. The cover of the book was funny, and the title was humorous and intriguing. The opening lines of the book were light and amusing. They revealed character, posed questions and implied this was going to be a funny story. But instead of being the comic novel the cover, title, tone and opening promised, the story turned dark and troubled. My son not only resented this literary double-dealing, he made a point never to read another book written by that author.

That alone should be reason enough for you to honor the original promise you make to your reader.

I hasten to add that having the narrator tell the story in a funny voice and contrasting it with a menacing tone is not the same thing as misleading the reader. Humor isn't the problem; how the whole book is presented to the reader is the problem.

THEME AND PREMISE

Lots of people confuse theme and premise. This is easy to do since the two are kissing cousins and will blur if you so much as blow on them. It's a good idea, however, to distinguish these concepts in your mind. Making this effort will not only help you construct your plot, it will help you keep your story on track.

Premise

The word "premise" is derived from Medieval Latin. "Missa" or "misse" means put. And "pre" means before. To put before.

Premise, as James N. Frey defines it in *How to Write a Damn Good Novel*, is "a statement of what happens to the characters as a result of the actions of a story. . . . Does every dramatic story have a premise? Yes. One and only one premise? Yes. You can't ride two bicycles at the same time and you can't prove two premises at the same time."

The premise of *The Three Little Pigs* is not three innocents threatened by a scary monster. Nor is it the merits of various construction techniques in middle-income housing. The premise, Frey says, is "Foolishness leads to death and wisdom leads to happiness."

Another example of premise can be found in one of Aesop's Fables. A crow manages to snag a piece of cheese and settle on the branch of a tree to eat it. But when a fox sees the cheese, he wants that tasty morsel for himself. Living up to his wily reputation, the fox convinces the crow he wants to hear her sing. Succumbing to flattery, the crow opens her mouth and begins to caw, and the cheese falls into the hands of the fox.

The premise? If you can't get what you want by asking, you can get it by flattering. The fable demonstrates this premise in its actions.

The premise is what your book is about. Premise is not the plot. It is the *underlying idea* that supports the plot. Ideally, you should establish the premise of your story before you even begin writing. If you can do this, you will save yourself untold creative angst.

Once you clarify what the premise of your book is, you can build your story on that foundation. (Premise, of course, also refers to property—an expression evolved from the reference to that which is put at the beginning of a legal document. Because we are building a story on a premise, for our purposes, we can use this second meaning as a visual reminder of what we're doing.)

Think of premise as the foundation of your plot, the essential truth you want to convey. Premise is the truth that gives shape to your story and meaning to the lives of your characters. Premise has a beginning—an idea—but it also has an ending—a conclusion. Before you begin to write your book, determine what your premise is and then build your story around it.

Premise: A life of petty crime leads to a life in prison.

Premise: Transforming a life takes a lifetime of work.

Premise: Where there's a will there's a way.

Premise: The first love you have is the last love you remember.

Premise: When you betray a friend, you lose a friend.

Premise: When you lose a friend, you lose your history.

You might not believe it's worth wasting your time to ponder the meaning and ramifications of premise. But if you think of premise as the most fundamental idea in your book that must be proven by the actions of your characters, it becomes clear that the premise is the underlying glue that binds your story together. It also keeps your plot on track and prevents it from falling apart.

James N. Frey says, "every good premise should contain an element of *character* which through *conflict* leads to a *conclusion*. . . . A dramatic story is the transformation of character through crisis; the premise is a succinct statement of that transformation."

If your protagonist "tells" you he must take a certain action, ask yourself if his behavior proves the premise. If your hero does something totally out of character, ask yourself if you can find a way to make this behavior reflect your premise.

Try defining the premise of your story in one sentence.

For instance, the premise of *Where the Wild Things Are* is when you learn to confront your monsters, it's possible to tame them.

The premise of *Harry Potter and the Sorcerer's Stone* is just when you think you know who you are and where you're going, life will step in and surprise you.

The key to establishing your premise is to focus on one idea and build your story around it.

Once you have the premise clearly set in your mind, you can plot your story to prove that premise. If you do not honor this concept, you run the risk of your story wandering in too many directions because it lacks the connective tissue the premise provides.

Theme

The theme of your book is the narrative concept behind your story, the idea explored within the context of what your book is about. The theme is *not* the premise. Nor is it the message or the moral.

One theme of a book might be the tug-of-war between love and hate. Another might be the exploration of what makes a girl courageous or how you draw the line between loyalty and betrayal.

Lots of books have more than one theme. In *Bridge to Terabithia*,

Katherine Paterson tells the tale of an unlikely bond forged between fourth grader Jess Aarons and his friend Leslie Burke. They form a deep and abiding friendship that binds them together forever. Although this friendship ends in tragedy, Jess is left with a new understanding of the depth of love and the importance of beauty and dreams.

The premise of this book is when we honor imagination, we honor life. In contrast to the premise, the themes of this book are the transcendent might of friendship, the transforming power of love, the untapped courage to do what is right and the heroic struggle to reconcile the awful reality of death with the persistent demands of life. These themes are represented in the behavior of the characters and the elements of the plot.

Theme is not a one-sided reflection of a character or situation. Theme has multiple dimensions and is developed in multiple ways—light and dark, inside and outside, upside down and right side up. One theme echoes an earlier theme. One theme evolves from another.

When a composer writes variations on a theme, at one moment the melody might be picked up by a cello; the next moment it's echoed by a trumpet. The melody then shifts into a minor key and is presented all over again by the full orchestra. Three different sounds, three different ways of listening to the same musical theme. Three different versions of the same song.

A literary theme is developed in a similar way, in repeated echoes and variations on the original. In one scene we might write about love and redemption in a positive light. Then we shift to the flip side, the dark side of love manifested in obsession, possession and death.

Joy, vision, strength, weakness, creativity, disappointment, longing, rejection, fantasy, love, loss, fear, grief, death, hope. Whether you're writing for children or adults, all the aspects of our lives and our behavior that are an integral part of the human condition become transformed into themes in the hands of a writer.

The Moral of the Story. A moral is a lesson, a teaching. In storytelling, the moral often involves overtly judging the good or bad behavior of one or more of the characters—a lesson directed specifically at the reader. And the moral of this story is . . .

If you look at the moral of the story as a quality exemplified in the behavior and attitudes of a character, then of course you can include it in a story. However, a moral steeped in sermonizing is a major no-no.

My one-word advice to anyone who sets out to write a story with a stated moral is: don't. Aesop could get away with it; we can't. Theme is not a moral. Premise is not a moral. And a moral is not a moral, either. It's a pain in the wazoo.

As I said earlier, if kids so much as get a faint whiff you are preaching to them, they will deposit your book on the nearest shelf faster than a speeding bullet.

This doesn't preclude your ability to impart specific ideas in your book, any more than it precludes your ability to convey the fact that there are consequences to the decisions we make. But you must communicate these ideas through the actions and reactions of characters, and not through the author preaching to the reader or one character preaching to another. In short, if you ditch the preaching you can keep the message.

BACKGROUND COLORS

Promise, premise and theme. In and of themselves, these issues seem insignificant compared to the challenge of structuring and writing an entire book. But it is these very issues—the subtleties that indicate a writer is in full command of her work—that lift your story above the crowd and make it a book to respect and remember.

Your Turn
Keeping Your Word

1) Choose your three favorite children's books. Then ask yourself the following questions.

- What is the promise the writer makes to the reader? How does the author make that promise?

- What is the premise of the book? Define this in one sentence. How do the characters reflect this premise?

- What are the themes of the book? How are these themes expressed?

2) Once you have analyzed these books, take the book you're working on or that you intend to write. Review the following checklist, and apply these items to your own project.

- Make certain your premise is set firmly in your mind.
- Evaluate the promise you make to your reader.
- Analyze how the actions and feelings of your characters reflect your premise.
- Define the themes of your story and how they are manifested in the actions of your characters and the elements of the plot.
- Remove all traces of any moral or lesson you feel compelled to teach.

CHAPTER SEVENTEEN

The Promise Continued: Voice and Tone

A strong narrative voice creates a feeling in the reader that the writer knows what he or she is talking about. It creates trust.

—James N. Frey, How to Write a Damn Good Novel, II

OTHER VOICES, OTHER TONES

To the casual observer, voice and tone are one and the same. Like those pesky kissing cousins premise and theme, voice and tone are interconnected and often function more as twins than as cousins. Occasionally, they even behave like siblings, mirroring each other one minute and conflicting with each other the next. Both, however, contribute to the art of storytelling and shape the promise you make to your reader.

Boiled down to their essence, voice and tone can be defined in the following way.

• *Voice:* The quality of the narration, regardless of whether it's told in first or third person.

• *Tone:* The atmosphere of the book.

Working with these definitions, let's examine each narrative feature separately.

VOICE LESSONS

Now that you have a handle on the structural picture of your book, it's time to decide how you're going to tell your story. This is your chance to become someone else, to put on a mask and become a clown, to experience what it's like to live in the skin of the opposite sex or live in the dark heart of a stranger.

The voice you choose to write with will either belong to the narrator or to a character in the book. You've got lots of options. Do you want to be ironic or comic? Serious, detached or entertaining? Take a look at these opening sentences and how they establish the voice.

Here, the author writes with a plain, tough-guy edge.

> You wouldn't think we'd have to leave Chicago to see a dead body. We were growing up there back in the bad old days of Al Capone and Bugs Moran. Just the winter before, they'd had the St. Valentine's Day Massacre over on North Clark Street. The city had such an evil reputation that the Thompson submachine gun was better know as a "Chicago typewriter."
>
> —Richard Peck, *A Long Way From Chicago*

A more formal voice is often used in fantasy, with the author choosing old-fashioned words and phrases to transport the reader into a different mind-set.

> Lyra and her daemon moved through the darkening hall, taking care to keep to one side, out of sight of the kitchen. The three great tables that ran the length of the hall were laid already, the silver and the glass catching what little light there was, and the long benches were pulled out ready for the guests. Portraits of former Masters hung high up in the gloom along the walls.
>
> —Philip Pullman, *The Golden Compass*

A comic story has a lighter, more casual voice.

> "Mom, I hate these sneakers." Richard Bickerstaff was getting dressed for school.

"You picked them out yourself last week, sweetie," his mother called from the kitchen.

"Last week they were okay. Today I hate them."

—Jonathan Etra and Stephanie Spinner, *Aliens for Breakfast*

A serious novel combines various styles to create a narrative voice that fits a more somber mood.

They murdered him.

As he turned to take the ball, a dam burst against the side of his head and a hand grenade shattered his stomach. Engulfed by nausea, he pitched toward the grass. His mouth encountered gravel, and he spat frantically, afraid that some of his teeth had been knocked out.

—Robert Cormier, *The Chocolate War*

A novel infused with parody has another voice.

I, Artemis Bonner, in order to get my side of the story on record, and to explain why I am going to kill a low-lifed and sniveling scoundrel called by the name of Catfish Grimes, am writing down my side of the story so the real truth is known. I do not want anyone to think, when the time comes, that Catfish died by accident or by the hand of a stranger. It was me, Artemis Bonner, who has done the deed.

—Walter Dean Myers, *The Righteous Revenge of Artemis Bonner*

A detective novel has a distinctive, Raymond Chandler-like voice all its own.

Some cases start rough, some cases start easy. This one started with a dame. (That's what we private eyes call a girl.)

It was a hot day in September. The kind of day when kindergartners wake up cranky from their naps. The kind of day

when teachers pull their hair and dream of moving to
Antarctica.
—Bruce Hale, *The Chameleon Wore Chartreuse*

Whether the stories are told in first or third person, all of these books
are written in a voice that enhances the story, a voice tailor-made for
the subject. Each voice is strong, and each voice is unique.

A first-person voice is easier to individualize than a third-person voice.
When considering the latter, there's no shortage of advice to writers
about how the narrator of a book should disappear or assume the form
of another posy in the flowered fictional wallpaper. Balderdash! Some
of the most memorable books you read—the ones that stay with you
long after you have closed the covers—have a unique narrative voice.

Instead of trying to make the narrator disappear, think of this third-
person voice as another character in your book. Some characters like to
occupy center stage; others hang out in the wings. But they each have
a distinct and necessary presence. Just as each character speaks in an
individual voice, so do you. And the voice you write with will influence
how the reader feels about the story.

Vocal Consistency

In fiction, consistency of voice is critical. Even though you're ironic one
minute and innocent the next, your reader should be able to depend on
your narrative voice remaining essentially the same throughout the
story. Indiscriminate mixing and matching—fantasy voice here, Sam
Spade voice there—will confuse the reader and most likely cause him
to lose interest in your story. This idea especially holds true for younger
readers.

Musical Voices

Although this book you're reading isn't fiction, it is written in a distinct
voice. At least I hope it is. Even though I am serious in one section,
philosophical in another, and—I hope—amusing in another, the voice
I'm using is open and informal. Helpful information mixed with opinion, spiced with humor, seasoned with friendly persuasion and steeped
in the down-home juices of my Oklahoma roots. Come on in. Sit down,

make yourself at home. Let's talk about how to write a story. And let's have some fun doing it. That's my voice; the one I've chosen to write this book.

But this is not the voice I use in all my books. Each project is different. Each story, fiction or nonfiction, demands its own voice.

One April Morning is the nonfiction book I wrote for children about the Oklahoma City bombing. Out of respect for the subject matter and the variety of voices used in the story, I kept my narrative voice consistent. I told the story in a reportorial free verse, then contrasted my own words with the words of the children—ages three to fifteen—I interviewed. I deliberately chose a more distanced voice so it would stand apart from the poignancy of the children's voices. Their observations served as a Greek chorus—a collective voice—that commented on the action and amplified the more traditional description of the tragedy they had experienced.

Firefighters and police officers, priests and
parents,
doctors and nurses, friends and strangers,
rushed to the scene of the blast.
Wails of sirens drowned out cries for help
as injured people, dazed and bleeding,
wandered from the bombed-out buildings.
Others, less fortunate, were trapped inside.
At hospitals all over the city, emergency teams
assembled
to await the arrival of the wounded.

"My mommy was at her hospital," said Gracie.
"She was looking out for all the people."
"My daddy is a doctor. He went to his hospital,"
said Rachel.
"He waited and waited for someone he could help.
But nobody came because most of the people were
dead."
"There were parents walking around outside the

> *building with pictures of their kids, asking if any-*
> *body had seen them," said Brad.*
> *"I was scared," said Melissa, "because my mom*
> *was downtown."*
> *"I was scared," said Brendon. "My guts were scared*
> *and I was trying to hide somewhere."*
>
> Stronger than a hurricane wind,
> louder than crashing thunder,
> the helter-skelter bomb blast even blew away
> the clothes that people wore.
>
> *"My daddy got a two-year-old baby out of the*
> *ambulance,"*
> *said Addi. "It only had socks on."*

Because the details of the bombing were familiar to most people from magazine, television and newspaper accounts, I needed to find a different way to tell the story, a way unfamiliar to readers. In this case, I created two "voices" to play off each other—just one of many approaches to storytelling.

Finding Your Voice

Every book has a story. And every story has a voice. Creating the right interplay between these two elements is critical.

Different projects, different voices. They're all inside you. The catch is, in order for you to find your true voice you're going to have to shed your old one. The school voice. The please-the-teacher voice. The term-paper-in-college voice.

A few years ago I took the exam to enable me to teach in Los Angeles schools. It probably comes as no surprise that in order to pass the test, I had to take a brush-up course in math, especially algebra. Definitely not my strong suit. Never was, never will be. I still get a glitch in my stomach when I hear a sentence that begins with, "If a train leaves Chicago traveling at sixty miles an hour . . ."

I've never been good at taking tests. But other than to refresh my memory about how to structure a formal essay, I didn't worry about the writing portion of the teacher's exam. After all, I had published thirty-nine books. I didn't need a refresher course in writing.

Big mistake.

Big, big mistake.

I did fine on the math section of the test, but I blew the writing. Truth be told, I fell into the "needs work" category, the last stop on the examination line before failure. That's because I had to write three short, formal essays on assigned topics in thirty minutes. Ten minutes per essay. No extra time allowed.

Fifteen minutes into the half hour, I was still trying to formulate what I was going to say, how I was going to approach the subjects, which way I was going to express the thoughts and in what tone of voice I was going to write.

I wanted to say something interesting, insightful and creative, perhaps even amusing. And I wanted to say it well.

All the examiners wanted, however, was adequate prose with a well-constructed topic sentence, a couple of supporting statements and a conclusion. What more can you expect in a ten-minute essay? The judges didn't care if the essay was creative. They didn't care if I used interesting words or presented the material in a unique or memorable way. They just wanted to know I was proficient in the basics of writing, while I wanted to know I had created an intriguing essay. In the process of trying to reach my goal, I came perilously close to running out of time and failing the exam.

I had been writing books for years. I had long ago shed my school voice, and it never occurred to me to go back to it. Other than almost failing the teacher exam, I don't regret for a minute leaving my academic voice in the literary dust. With a little effort, I suppose I could resurrect the voice with which I wrote term papers in college. The voice that demonstrates good grammar, grasp of subject and clear use of language—but that has no color, no passion and no originality.

As in:

In addressing the complex conundrum of the split literary personality, there are two distinct styles the student of writing might choose to emulate. Although the dual options are diametrically opposed, each occupies a valid place within the demanding context of the literary and academic landscape.

One: Learn to write in an efficient and timely manner in whole sentences and adequate prose. Remember to stick in a ten dollar word every now and then.

Two: Forget the above, invoke your literary muse and find the voice within you.

In other words, before you write for a wider audience, it's important for you to shed your school voice and find a richer, more authentic way to express yourself. Take the time and make the effort to discover the voice that belongs to *you*, not to your third-grade social studies teacher or your college English professor. The voice that comes from the naked core of truth that lives deep inside us all.

Once you discover the authenticity within yourself, you can move into all the other voices that inhabit your imagination with an assurance you never before experienced. This is, after all, the way you honor your essential self and elevate your creative spirit. It is also a way to reclaim the enchantment of mind that is your original nature and your birthright.

TONE

Beyond the voice you choose to tell your story, you also convey your promise to the reader by the tone—the atmosphere—you create.

Are you writing a book that's light and fun to read? Your tone should reflect this. Paula Danziger achieves this goal in the opening sentences of *Everyone Else's Parents Said Yes*. The style is casual, the subject matter is amusing, and the hero is quirky. The author's tone reflects this mood in the outrageous precision of Matthew's words and the detailed explanation that follows.

"Mom. You know there are only five more days, fifteen hours, and thirty-two minutes until my birthday party." Matthew Martin enters the kitchen holding a computer printout.

Matthew Martin can be very organized and accurate when he wants to be, and he wants to be. Since he's the youngest person in his sixth-grade class, birthdays really count.

In *Killing Mr. Griffin*, Lois Duncan's novel about the confrontation between good and evil in the high school arena, she begins her book with a dynamic opening sentence. In just seventeen words, the author conveys a dark purpose to the story and a sense that the world is out of whack.

It was a wild, windy southwestern spring when the idea of killing Mr. Griffin occurred to them.

Already the reader knows this is the beginning of an ugly, tension-filled story. In one sentence that foreshadows group mayhem, we know something dreadful is about to happen. This is what Duncan promises with her opening declaration. And this is what she delivers.

On the other hand, if you want to write a tantalizing and thought-provoking story, your tone should reflect this feeling. Jerry Spinelli begins *Maniac Magee* with:

They say Maniac Magee was born in a dump. They say his stomach was a cereal box and his heart a sofa spring.

They say he kept an eight-inch cockroach on a leash and that rats stood guard over him while he slept.

They say if you knew he was coming and you sprinkled salt on the ground and he ran over it, within two or three blocks he would be as slow as everybody else.

They say.

What's true, what's myth? It's hard to know.

Here, the author's deliberate tone reflects the mythic character of Maniac. This careful and calculated technique, combined with the use of the mysterious "they," evokes numerous questions in the reader's mind. Questions that demand an answer.

Tone, then, is the atmosphere created by the author's reflection of the events in the book. For instance, Spinelli uses terse words and short sentences. I could tell the same story and say the same things and totally change the tone of the book. For instance:

> Some kids say Maniac Magee was born in a dump and that his stomach's like a cereal box and his heart looks like a sofa spring.
>
> Maniac's next door neighbor claims he keeps an eight-inch cockroach on a leash and he's guarded by rats when he sleeps.
>
> As if that's not enough, some kids say, "If you know Maniac's coming, and you sprinkle salt on the ground and he runs over it, he'll turn into a regular runner just like every-body else."
>
> Sometimes it's really hard to figure out what's true and what isn't.

Even though I've said essentially the same thing as Spinelli, how I've said it—longer sentences, softer phrases, the removal of the mysterious "they"—changes the tone of the story from compelling to boring and destroys a powerful opening to an unforgettable book.

The tone of your book depends on the words you choose. Consider the rhythm of your sentences, the sound of the language and the way these elements are combined. Short, terse words and phrases convey an entirely different mood than longer words and sentences.

Think of tone as paint. Just as you create different moods in a room when you paint the walls different colors, the language you choose creates different moods in your story. Take advantage of the verbal palette in your command. Your story will be stronger for the effort.

SIBLINGS

Your voice and tone tell the reader your book is a mystery, a romance, a thriller, a historical tale, a time-travel adventure or a coming-of-age story. You tell him this is a comic novel, a serious novel or a tragic novel. Sometimes voice and tone are the same. In *Don't Call Me Beanhead!* Susan Wojciechowski begins her tale with:

> My teacher, Ms. Babbit, wears a different pair of earrings practically every day. She has heart earrings for Valentine's Day, pumpkins for Halloween, turkeys for Thanksgiving, candy canes for Christmas.

Wojciechowski has used an amusing voice to create an amusing tone to the story. Here, the two elements blend.

Sometimes, however, voice and tone work at deliberate cross-purposes, as in Chris Crutcher's *Chinese Handcuffs*. In the prologue of the book, the hero is competing in a triathlon.

> Dillon stumbles across the finish line and falls to the side of the path, onto the cool grass, where he lies there on his back, in immense pain, laughing and forcing his toes back toward his shins to hold off the dancing cramp muscles in his legs.
>
> "Keep walking," an official says kindly. "Keep walking or we'll need a rack to stretch your legs out."
>
> Dillon nods, trying to rise, but the cramps bring him to the ground. He laughs to keep from crying and says, "Shoot me," to the official. "Please. Shoot me."
>
> The official smiles and walks away.
>
> "Not to end the pain," Dillon yells after him. "To end the stupidity."

Here, the voice of the narrator is colored with an edgy humor that stands in stark contrast to the dark circumstances of the story. Dillon laughs at himself and jokes with the official. But he is in serious psychic pain.

Chinese Handcuffs is the dark and gripping tale of two teenagers trying to survive the emotional fallout from horrific encounters with cruelty and despair. Dillon has witnessed the suicide of his brother, and his friend Jenn has been molested by her father and stepfather. The hero's use of humor helps him maintain a buffer between the ordinary events of his life and the demons that haunt him, just as the book's author maintains a contrast between the dark humor of the voice and tragic tone of the book.

Setting tone and voice against each other is a powerful and effective narrative technique. For instance, if you want to tell a ghost story, you don't begin with a hero who's a woo-woo kind of guy. You begin with a just-the-facts, ma'am, show-me-or-it-doesn't-exist kind of fellow, and you reflect this in the narrative voice you choose and the way the hero speaks. Short sentences. Strong words. Clear thoughts. After establishing the hero's down-to-earth character in the reader's mind, his stunned reaction when he sees the ghost then becomes instantly believable.

How do you accomplish this dual technique? You write your story in first or third person, and you speak with a no-nonsense, matter-of-fact voice. Then you pull the rug out from under this sensible, rational presentation by creating a threatening tone, remembering always that what you don't see is scarier than what you do.

You can use voice and tone as twins that work in tandem to reflect each other, or you can divide them and use them as distant relations that contrast with each other. It all depends on the story you want to tell and the demands the story makes. With careful planning, these two elements become powerful tools in the writer's story-telling arsenal.

Your Turn
Finding the Right Notes

Write the opening paragraphs of a story about an adolescent girl and her adventures on an ill-fated camping trip.

Voice

1) Tell the same story in the following first-person voices.

• A teenager relating the story to some kids at school.

• Mrs. Vandermeer, dripping in jewels, talking to a friend.

• A parent who overhears what happened on the trip.

• The school guidance counselor.

2) Now choose a third-person narrative voice and tell the same story to the following people.

• Kids around a campfire in upbeat tone.

• A best friend in gossipy tone.

• A stranger on a plane in intimate tone.

3) Ask yourself the following questions.

• How would you alter your words and voice to suit the situation?

• What would you say to one group that you wouldn't to another?

• How would you interact with the different people?

• Would you confide more incriminating details to a stranger than a friend?

Tone

1) Choose the paragraphs from the examples in this chapter, and re-write them in different tones.

• Write *Everyone Else's Parents Said Yes* in a serious tone.

• Write *Maniac McGee* in a breezy, lighthearted tone.

• Write *Don't Call Me Beanhead!* in a formal tone.

• Write *The Chameleon Wore Chartreuse* in a neutral tone.

2) In order to accomplish this, consider the following questions.

• What changes in vocabulary are necessary to create the transformation you want to make?

• How can you use contractions to shift from a formal to a casual style?

• How can you shift points of view to create a different tone in the same story?

• What do you need to do to slip into the skin of a character?

• How does varying the length of the sentences create a soft or a tough tone?

3) Finally, ask yourself how you could change the voice and tone in the story you are working on.

- Is there a different tone you could use that would make your story stronger?
- Is there a different voice you could use that would make your story more compelling?
- Is there a way you could contrast voice and tone that would make your story more intriguing?

Don't be afraid to experiment and try on different narrative outfits. There's a chance you could find a more effective way to tell your story and more vital way to involve your reader.

CHAPTER EIGHTEEN

Narrative Authority: Setting and Senses

In every piece of fiction . . . setting is one of the three major elements—
along with characterization and plot—that the writer
must weave together to create the narrative.

—Connie C. Epstein, The Art of Writing for Children

ESTABLISHING AN ANCHOR

When I ghostwrote a book not long ago, the "author" sent me voluminous notes about incidents she wanted included in the book. Time and again I'd open my e-mail and find entries with phrases such as, "I met John William, a filmmaker, and he told me about . . . " or "When I sat down to talk with Katherine . . . " Again and again I would write back, "Where and when did you meet him? Where and when did you talk with her?" We had never encountered these people before, yet they had been given no anchor in time or place. As a consequence, they couldn't come to life.

An editor friend of mine calls this act of anchoring your story "narrative authority." By this, he means you must give the reader signposts along the way in order to maintain a sense of narrative continuity. Whether you're writing fiction or nonfiction, inserting a character or incident into a story without relating it to the rest of the book creates a sense of disconnection with the reader.

My point? *Specificity creates authenticity.*

The Five Ws

When we were in school, most of us learned the basics of journalism from our teachers. After talking to the class about the assignment at hand, the teacher would turn around and jot five words on the blackboard.

1) Who?
2) Where?
3) When?
4) What?
5) Why?

This may be old news, but it's as current as today's Web sites or the children's novel you are writing.

There are lots of ways to convey this information. You don't need to begin your book with, "It was in Chicago in 1942 that Smasher Malone looked at me one day, curled his fist and gave me a left cross on my jaw—all because he thought he was in love with the girl I took to the prom."

Granted, that opening answers all the w's, but it crams the information into a tight space. You can, of course, use the sentence as a jumping-off point, writing the story as a flashback leading up to the left cross to the jaw. On the other hand, you can mete out the information a little at a time. In fact, you could create an entire novel from the information in that one sentence.

Using this approach, you could string out your information in pieces. Like our old friends Hansel and Gretel dropping crumbs in the forest, you weave the information in and out of your narrative as you tell your story. You needn't sock it to the reader all at once.

For instance:

1) Who. The story begins in high school where the seventeen-year-old narrator named Jonas Chapnick and his best friend, Ted "Smasher" Malone, sit in English class together. They've known each other since second grade and now they're both looking at the same girl, and desiring her, as she stands in front of the room to read the poem she has written.

2) Where. Jonas glances out the window of the classroom and notes how dark clouds hang over Lake Michigan and the Chicago skyline.

3) When. The next Sunday afternoon, Jonas and Ted go to the movies. Afterwards, they walk outside, pulling their coats around them as the icy weather assaults their bodies. Then they hear the newspaper boy crying out, "Extra! Extra! Japanese attack Pearl Harbor!"

Cut to the following day when our hero sits in front of the radio with his mother, father and little sister. They listen to President Franklin Roosevelt as he says, "Yesterday, December 7, 1941—a date which will live in infamy—the United States of America was suddenly and deliberately attacked by naval and air forces of the Empire of Japan."

4) *What.* Two days later we follow Jonas and Ted as they try to enlist in the armed services at the naval recruiting station. They are rejected because they're too young, and they can't get the permission of their parents to join. They make a bet about who gets to fight the Nazis first.

5) *Why.* Tension begins to grow between the two boys as they wait until their eighteenth birthdays so they can join the army. They are both on the baseball team, and they both want to play shortstop. The competition between the boys builds as they both also try to date Diana, the girl who was reading the poem. When Jonas asks the object of their mutual affection to the prom before Ted, the split between the boys is complete.

Specificity

As you go through the story of rivalry, conflict and reconciliation, you anchor each new incident and each new encounter in time and place. Whether the scene occurs at a diner, the promenade along the lake or the high school baseball field, the reader needs to know where the characters are, what time it is—i.e., school gym, Friday, April—and how time and place relate to the larger story.

You can begin a paragraph with, "Tuesday evening, Jonas picked up his copy of *A Tale of Two Cities* and settled on his bed to read" or "The chilly April rain soaked through Ted's coat before he was a block from home." However you choose to anchor the story, young readers, especially, need to have consistent clues about where the hero is within the overall context of the narrative. Is he at home? At school? What for? When? Why?

Setting

There are lots of things you can do with setting. Setting adds color to the story. Setting affects characters. Setting lends authenticity to the narrative and paints pictures in the imaginations of readers. It's not enough to write about how cold Chicago is in the winter of 1942. You have to show us how the cold looks and feels and tastes.

Talk about how the icy wind blows off the lake and freezes car door locks or how icicles hang from the eaves of buildings and snow heaps in soft blankets over parked cars. Beyond the weather, facts about the life of the city lend authority to your narrative. Talk about the El, jazz joints, Marshall Field's, the White Sox, soldiers walking along the train tracks in Union Station. These are the details that lift your story into the realm of first-class fiction, the details that give your narrative both credibility and texture.

MAKING SENSE SENSE

French author Marcel Proust begins his seven-volume novel *Remembrance of Things Past* with the narrator of the story sharing tea with his mother and eating small sweet cakes called madeleines. Suddenly the scent of the madeleines transports the storyteller back to the long forgotten days of his youth. It is sense memory, not conscious recollection, that summons lost scenes from a shrouded past and finally exposes the meaning and significance of the narrator's childhood experience.

Certain "privileged moments" of memory, Proust posits, evoke hidden associations in our unconscious. This, in turn, allows us to exist simultaneously in both past and present—a fleeting transcendence of the limitations of time that permits us a glimpse of the essential truth common to both experiences.

For reader and writer, sensory details awaken sleeping thoughts and feelings, allowing our imaginations to exist in two places at once. The sight of a Model T Ford, the texture of velvet, the taste of rock salt or the sound of a lullaby create unexpected echoes in our imaginations. Specific sights and sensations evoke memories of other times and other places, memories we can use to create stories that move beyond authenticity into the heart of truth.

Think of your book as a living, organic entity. It breathes, it smells, it senses. It touches and tastes. Your job is to feed these senses, to keep them alive amidst the challenge and conflict and turmoil your hero must confront.

It's not enough to talk about how something looks or smells. Take the time to integrate this information with the character.

Before: The pungent scent of the baking bread penetrated the house.

After: The pungent scent of the baking bread penetrated the darkening corners of the house, invading Jonas' senses, reminding him he hadn't eaten since morning.

This kind of sensory detail not only describes the smell of the bread, it establishes the time of day and invites the reader into the mind and body of the hero of the story.

The Five Senses

Most of us are fortunate enough to be born with our five senses intact. Throughout our lives our experience feeds these senses. We develop likes and dislikes. We avoid some things, embrace others. Our senses enrich us at the same time they inform us.

When you write, keep all of these senses in mind. Here again is a list of things to trigger your memory and use as springboards for the sensory details you integrate into your own book. Add items to the list. Delete others. Tweak it, edit it, enhance it. Make the list your own.

1) Smell

❏ Laundry detergent	❏ Baking bread
❏ Roses	❏ Puppies
❏ Sneezy smells	❏ Car exhaust
❏ Roast beef cooking	❏ Wood-burning fire
❏ Sea breezes	❏ Mint
❏ Smoke	❏ Lemon
❏ Eucalyptus	❏ Fish
❏ Babies	❏ Incense
❏ Chili	

2) Sound

- ❏ Bach
- ❏ Willie Nelson
- ❏ Louis Armstrong
- ❏ Ella Fitzgerald
- ❏ Hymns
- ❏ Wind in the trees
- ❏ Ocean waves
- ❏ Water flowing from the tap
- ❏ Whispers
- ❏ Trumpets

- ❏ Tenors
- ❏ Mother's voice
- ❏ Baby's cry
- ❏ Movies
- ❏ Chalk on a blackboard
- ❏ Kitten's meow
- ❏ Rain on the roof
- ❏ Children playing
- ❏ Chimes

3) Sight

- ❏ Sunset
- ❏ Mountains
- ❏ Babies
- ❏ Kittens
- ❏ Puppies
- ❏ Garbage dump
- ❏ Father's face
- ❏ Birthday cake
- ❏ Ocean waves

- ❏ IRS notice
- ❏ Sailboat
- ❏ Red sports car
- ❏ Cartoon page
- ❏ Blue eyes
- ❏ New bike
- ❏ Christmas tree
- ❏ Bumper-to-bumper traffic

4) Touch

❏ Sandpaper	❏ Concrete wall
❏ Shag carpet	❏ Feathers
❏ Wooden banister	❏ Soil
❏ Cold water	❏ New book
❏ Hot stove	❏ Skateboard
❏ Muscles	❏ Worm
❏ Hair	❏ Soda can
❏ Bald head	❏ Silk and satin
❏ Buzz cut	❏ Caterpillar crawling on finger
❏ Orange rind	
❏ Baby's skin	❏ The worn velour of old teddy bear

5) Taste and Texture

❏ Salty (peanuts, chicken soup, potato chips)	❏ Hot (cinnamon, chilies, garlic)
❏ Sweet (brownies, ice cream, nectarines)	❏ Mushy (beans, mashed potatoes, liver)
❏ Bitter (arugula, cranberries, horseradish)	❏ Crunchy (cashews, carrots, toast)
❏ Sour (lemon, lime)	❏ Chewy (roast beef, gum, mozzarella cheese)

Warning!

The Devil's in the Details

It is possible to create too much of a good thing. Too much detail can destroy your story. Not long ago I edited a book that took place in America at the turn of the twentieth century. It was obvious the author did massive amounts of research in order to create a story that was authentic to time and place. Every last iota of information the writer knew about this historical period was integrated into the book. The overwhelming inclusion of architectural detail, cultural facts, thoughts, quotes, history, customs and costumes from the period drowned what was essentially an intriguing and well-plotted book.

If yours is a book that has required a lot of research, make certain your story doesn't take a back seat to the facts and figures you include. Otherwise, your narrative threads will be overwhelmed by details and your story will be lost along with your reader.

My point: Just because you have done massive amounts of research doesn't mean you should include it all in your book.

• *Consolation:* When you make the effort to do your research in order to be historically and culturally accurate, your time is never lost. Even if you don't use everything you've learned, the knowledge you've accumulated allows you to write with authority and authenticity. When it comes to research, treat it like salt. Use only what is necessary, and set aside the rest.

Your Turn
Sense and Sensibility

1) Write the opening pages of a book about an eleven-year-old girl living in the country who is sent to live with her aunt in New York City after her parents are killed in an accident. Choose a time period from your own youth. Incorporate the following sensory details in your account.

- The last sight of the farm where she grew up.
- The sensation of her first plane ride.
- The smell of a New York street in August.
- The disorientation the girl feels.
- The scent of her aunt's perfume.
- The familiar touch of her old bedspread.
- The memory of her mother singing "Hush, Little Baby."
- The taste of her tears.

2) After you've written this opening, go back to the book you are working on now. As you read and write, make certain you have accomplished the sense and setting goals discussed in this chapter. Questions to ask yourself as you read and write your own story:

- Are these details blended smoothly into the story?
- Are these details integrated into the character's experience?
- Are these details plausible?
- Do these details add texture to the story?
- Do these details add authenticity to the story?
- Do these details add to the story or detract from it?

If you can answer yes to all these questions, you're on the right track.

CHAPTER NINETEEN

The Write Way

When you catch an adjective, kill it.

—*Mark Twain*

LITTERBUG

When I first began to write, I thought adjectives and adverbs were honestly and truly fabulous, entrancing and enhancing. My overblown prose was virtually littered with these pesky parts of speech. It took me a long time to figure out that adjectives interfere with prose more often than they improve it and adverbs kill a sentence more often than they enliven it.

Some people are born with an understanding of good writing. They feel the rhythm and hear the music from the moment they set pen to paper. Most of us, however, aren't blessed with this natural gift. We lesser mortals must learn how to write—must practice our art and hone our craft as part of our daily discipline.

Have I Got a Gift for You!

It took me fifteen years to learn how to write. What a waste. I know now that it's not necessary to squander half your productive literary life hacking a path through a jungle of words in search of powerful prose. There's another way to master the craft.

Strong prose is a matter of practice and discipline and conscious aware-ness of the words you put on the page. There are rules for effective writing. If you apply the following principles every time you sit down to write, they'll become second nature.

These rules can't make a good writer a brilliant one. But they can make an average writer a good writer and a good writer a better writer. They can also turn a mediocre story into a notable one.

Nancy Lamb's Twenty-Six Steps to Good Writing

1) Never Let the Truth Get in the Way of Your Story. Creative writing is just that: creative. If the truth prevents you from telling your fictional story effectively, get rid of the facts and invent something that makes the story work.

2) Show Don't Tell. This is one of the most important rules of good writing. Don't tell me how someone feels. Show me.

The vampire was thrilled when he saw he was standing near the entrance to the blood bank.

Instead, write:

When the vampire read the sign that said Blood Bank, *he grinned and licked his lips.*

3) Never Use Two Words When One Word Will Do. Less is more. Choose one powerful word instead of two weaker ones.

Andrea stared at the horrible, writhing mass of snakes.

Instead, write:

Andrea stared at the writhing mass of snakes.

4) Use the Active Voice. The difference between adequate prose and good prose is the difference between the passive and active voice. Make certain that active verbs drive your prose.

There were a great number of dead bodies on the ground.

Instead, write:

Dead bodies littered the ground.

5) Avoid Purple Prose. Create a graveyard for all those once-beloved adverbs and adjectives. Save the strong words and bury the rest.

Tiffany Cerise smiled prettily, her beautiful, enticing, cat-green eyes dancing seductively with alluring and predatory fires.

Instead, write:

When Tiffany smiled, her eyes danced with predatory fires.

6) Use Parallel Construction. Parallel construction allows you to write in the most interesting, economical fashion by uniting phrases with a common construction.

The Vampire bared his teeth and then, raising his claws to sharpen them, he started licking his chops. "Gotcha!" he said with a grin.

Instead, write:

The Vampire bared his teeth, sharpened his claws and licked his chops. "Gotcha!" he said with a grin.

7) Keep Related Words Together. Linguistic studies have shown that most of us have a natural instinct for the placement of adjectives. We don't say, "I have a blue shiny car." Instead, we say, "I have a shiny blue car." The same principle should be applied to the sentences you write.

Frankenstein noticed a large blood stain in the rug that was in the middle.

Instead, write:

Frankenstein noticed a large blood stain in the middle of the rug.

8) Write With Nouns and Verbs, Not With Adjectives and Adverbs. Cultivate the use of strong verbs. They are the most powerful tools in a writer's arsenal.

Since the day Barbara met the werewolf, she felt very scared and frightened.

Instead, write:

Terror haunted Barbara's heart from the day she met the werewolf.

9) Avoid Qualifiers and Other Wimpy Words. What are these words that blunt meaning and weaken prose? Rather, a lot, almost, sort of, about, somewhat, very, little, feel, big, pretty, just, maybe, beautiful, nice, about, somewhat, extremely, partially. One small word can make a big difference.

State the fact. Don't equivocate. Don't dilute.

The teacher was very angry and dismayed when she read the report.

Instead, write:

The teacher was angry and dismayed when she read the report.

10) Don't Explain Too Much. Give your reader the benefit of the doubt and allow him to intuit the meaning of the dialogue, rather than read about it.

"I'm sorry," Peter said consolingly.

Instead, write:

"I'm sorry," said Peter.

11) Eliminate All Unnecessary "Thats." This is a simple trick that simplifies your construction and cleans up your prose.

Eliminate all the "thats" that you possibly can.

Instead, write:

Eliminate all the "thats" you possibly can.

12) Use Short Paragraphs. As I said before, long paragraphs exhaust the eye and intimidate the reader. Short paragraphs help maintain a reader's focus.

13) Write Cinematically. When you write, think visually. Language holds endless possibilities for a creative approach to expressing an idea.

Eddy Peters exemplified this when he wrote, "Not only does the English Language borrow words from other languages, it sometimes chases them down dark alleys, hits them over the head, and goes through their pockets." (p.s.—Note the parallel construction.)

14) Vary Your Sentences. All declarative sentences make for dull reading. Break up the monotony.

John walked to the closet. He opened the door. He took one look inside, and he screamed.

Instead, write:

John walked to the closet and opened the door. Taking one look inside, he screamed.

15) Use Interesting Contrasts. Like the owl on the beach, search for ways to combine things that don't belong together.

People loved him because he was a scoundrel and a hero.

16) Juxtapose Words and Ideas to Evoke Humor and Irony. As you write, look for opportunities to play with words and combine unlikely ideas.

I believe in the kindness of strangers and the existence of evil.

and

The class president is a kid who lurches before he leaps.

17) Create Interest By Mixing Alien Ideas and Drawing Unlikely Parallels.
She was the kind of girl who collected boys like she collected speeding tickets. They both just happened.

18) Shun Adverbs. There's no surer way to weaken your prose than to pepper it with adverbs. In fact, these pesky parts of speech are so loathed by professional writers, I know of one poetry teacher in Los Angeles who insists that his students contribute five dollars to the class party fund for every adverb they use.

There are, of course, times when the adverb is appropriate and necessary. Choose those times carefully.

She looked longingly and lovingly at the chocolate.

or

She looked at the chocolate with longing and love.

or better

Her eyes consumed the chocolate.

19) *Avoid Highfalutin' Words.* Don't use a ten-dollar word when a five-dollar word will do. Big words don't make your prose sound more intelligent; they make it sound pretentious and unprofessional. Utilize *or* use, transpire *or* happen, automobile *or* car—choose the simple word.

20) *Listen to the Music.* Just as in poetry, the best prose has a rhythm to it. Honor that rhythm. There have been days when I've spent half an hour searching the thesaurus for a word that has three syllables instead of two. Sometimes the difference is subtle, but it is also effective.

Some writers catch onto the rhythm, and they delight in the sound of the music as soon as they learn to write.

Instead, write:

Some writers feel the rhythm and hear the music from the moment they learn to write.

21) *Watch Out for Word Repetition.* There's nothing more tiresome for a reader than seeing the same tiresome words over and over in the same paragraph. This creates the overall impression the reader is reading the same repetitive, tiresome prose over again, and it tires out the reader.

Note: The exception to this rule—the critical exception—is when you repeat a word for emphasis.

22) *Beware of "It."* Grammarians call it an "obscure pronominal reference." That's when "it" is left dangling in a sentence without a clear reference about who or what it refers to. Your reader should be able to follow it without having to reread it in an effort to figure out what it is saying or referring to. Got it?

23) *Write Sentences in the Positive Form.* This one's simple enough. Cast your sentences in the positive rather than the negative. Borrowing from *The Elements of Style* by William Strunk, Jr. and E.B. White:

Instead of: *When it came to appointments, she was not a prompt person.*

Write: *She was chronically late to her appointments.*

Not honest vs. dishonest

Not important vs. trifling

Did not remember vs. forgot

Did not pay attention vs. ignored

Did not have much confidence in vs. distrusted

24) *Learn to Use, Not Abuse, Metaphor and Simile.* Metaphor and simile are similar, in that they both delineate comparisons between unlike things.

To quote from Constance Hale's *Sin and Syntax: How to Craft Wickedly Effective Prose,* "In metaphor the comparison is expressed when a figurative term is substituted for a literal term."

When Shakespeare says, "All the world's a stage," he is using metaphor.

In simile, the comparison is expressed with words such as like, as and similar to.

When Robert Burns says, "O, my Luve is like a red, red rose," he is using simile.

Both of these literary devices lend power and substance to your writing. If you overuse them, however, they will lend tedium to the same writing.

25) *Write. Rewrite. Rewrite.* Before: There are transcendent moments in a writer's life when a paragraph or a page she or he writes is perfect the first time it is written. Trust me: These moments are as rare as rain in the Sahara. Most well-regarded prose is rewritten, reworked and re-edited.

After: There are transcendent moments in a writer's life when a paragraph or page is perfect the first time it is written. These moments are rare as rain in the Sahara. Most strong prose is rewritten, reworked and re-edited prose.

26) *There's an Exception to Every Rule.* Just because I write in absolutes and sound as if I know what I'm talking about, that doesn't mean these rules are carved in stone. What it does mean is I'm right 93.7 percent of the time. The other 6.3 percent falls under the rubric of exception to the rule. Your job is to learn to tell which is which by reading good prose, practicing your writing and increasing your awareness.

EDITORIAL PET PEEVES

In order to avoid annoying some overworked editor with usage errors and grammatical gaffes—or worse, giving her an excuse to turn down your manuscript—here are some language fundamentals every writer should know. Pay attention to them. These nit-picking points can define the distinction between professional and amateur writing.

I hasten to add that the following peeves are just the tip of the verbal boo-boo iceberg. Every writer should make the effort to use clear, concise language that honors words and meanings by using them correctly.

Top Ten Rules of Verbal Combat

1) Alright vs. All Right. To put it succinctly, the former is wrong, the latter is right.

It is not all right to spell all right alright.

2) Less vs. Few. Less refers to quality, few refers to quantity.

There is less frost on the pumpkins this year, but there are fewer pumpkins in the patch.

3) Presently vs. Currently. Presently means in a little while. Currently means now. Presently never means currently.

The president is currently busy, but she will be with you presently.

4) Loan vs. Lend. Loan is a noun; lend is a verb.

Mary told Bert she would be happy to lend him the money to pay his loan.

5) Me vs. I. Me and I are both pronouns. I is always a subject; me is always an object.

The prize money was sent to my dog and me. It was never never never sent to my dog and I. Furthermore, this secret windfall must remain between you and me, never between you and I.

An easy way to remember this is to take out the other person and rephrase the sentence. "The money was sent to I" certainly doesn't sound right. Neither does "between I and you."

6) He/She vs. Him/Her. Just as in me vs. I, there are lots of writers and speakers who confuse these words, including President George W. Bush who said, "You teach a child to read, and he or her will be able to pass the literary test."

To clarify: He and she are pronouns. Him and her are used as objects of a verb or a preposition.

Simon gave the book to him and her. He would never give the book to she and he. Nor would Simon give the book to he and I, or she and I.

Simon would, however, give the book to her and me, or him and me.

Furthermore, him and I don't go to the movies. Her and he don't hold hands in the movies. Nor do he and her do anything anywhere anyhow. But she and he and I can do anything we want.

7) Among vs. Between. Generally speaking, between is used when referring to two objects; among when referring to more than two.

Since the choice is between good and evil, I don't need to worry about choosing among the many behavioral shades of gray.

8) Each Other vs. One Another. Although lots of reputable writers break this rule, each other generally refers to two people, one another to more than two.

The twins torment each other constantly. The quadruplets get along with one another most of the time.

9) Lie vs. Lay. This one's a biggie, a peeve that ranks high on my personal best list. To wit: Lie, lay and lain are intransitive verbs. They take no object. Lay, laid and lain are transitive verbs that take an object. In other words, chickens lay eggs (the objects), people do not.

Today I lie on the beach. Yesterday I lay on the beach. I have also lain on the beach.

Today I lay the book on the table. Yesterday I laid the book on the table. I have also lain the book on the table.

I never never never lay on the beach or the couch or the bed or the floor— or anywhere else, for that matter. I don't lie the book on the table, either.

10) Farther vs. Further. Farther refers to distance. Further refers to time or quantity.

I can throw the ball farther than you. But you can pursue this contest further if you wish.

FINAL NOTE

There are scads of fine points about style and usage that should be mastered by anyone who is serious about writing, and there are scads of books written about this subject. I'm still a student of language, and I always will be. I learn new stuff all the time.

For a basic understanding of constructing prose, however, I suggest you invest in a copy of William Strunk, Jr. and E.B. White's *The Elements of Style*, first published in 1935. It's been revised over the years to keep up with the times, but it is still the holy bible of writing and style.

For a hip, contemporary guide to language and writing, read Constance Hale's *Sin and Syntax*. Hale's humor and intelligence are marvels of wisdom and common sense. Her text will make a better writer of anyone who reads it.

Both of these books amuse while they instruct, and both are worth reading and referring to regularly.

Your Turn

Tear and Compare

Take the opening chapter of your book. Go through it sentence by sentence, and apply the "Twenty-Six Steps to Good Writing" to your own prose. Do this even if you disagree with some of the rules and you think I'm full of verbal baloney.

- Once you have changed the chapter, compare the old version with the new.

- Ask yourself which one is stronger.

- If you belong to a writers critique group or have writer friends who are willing to read your pages, show the chapter to them. Ask them which version they prefer.

- Finally, apply what you have learned to the rest of your book.

Finishing
Touches

Coming Unglued

*It often seems to me that the biggest single issue for a writer
is how to stay buoyant enough to go on writing. How not to drown.*

—Janette Turner Hospital

EMERGENCY! EMERGENCY!

In writing, as in life, there are moments when our confidence disappears
and our courage fades, when staying afloat is all we can manage. This
loss of heart can happen to the strongest soul. Nobody is immune to
the crisis of faith. Nobody is exempt from the confrontation with failure.

William Butler Yeats describes this agony of mind in his poem, "The
Second Coming." "Things fall apart; the centre cannot hold; Mere anar-
chy is loosed upon the world." Our world.

For writers, this disintegration often comes dressed in the clothing of
an inability to put words on the page. Some people call it writer's block.
Some people look the other way and pretend they don't see the elephant
in the living room. Others immerse themselves in organizing their files
or cleaning their closets—or, like me, they indulge in a prolonged period
of procrastination. There's always another errand to run, another ap-
pointment to keep.

If you haven't yet reached this crisis point in your writing career, be
grateful for the blessing. Just know that if it ever does happen, there is
something you can do about it.

The Big Ugly

I don't want to dwell on this subject at length. The superstitious part of me chooses not to invest too much power in this state of mind. But I do want to offer some practical suggestions should you ever find yourself stuck in this bewildering place.

Eight Ways to Find Your Way Home

1) Make a List of Reasons Why You Love the Story. Why is this story worth writing? What makes the hero special? How does this story speak to you? How does it speak to your audience? Whose life will this story touch? What is it about this story that made you want to write it in the first place?

2) Skip the Section That's Giving You Trouble, and Write a Different Part of the Book. Who says you have to write a book in order? You know how the story begins. There's a good chance you know how it ends. If you're stuck in the beginning, skip to the middle or the end. If you're stuck in the middle, skip to the end. Wait until later to fill in the blanks.

3) Put the Book Away for Ten Days. "Forget" about the book. No matter how much you want to look at the manuscript, don't touch it. Don't even peek. Let the book float in your unconscious while you go to work, take walks, indulge in creative naps or catch up on all the chores you've been neglecting. Then return to the story refreshed.

4) Keep a Daily Journal About the Book. Spend three days not working on the book. Instead, make notes on characters and plot points. Write down ideas. Explore new ways to express your premise and themes. Take the Zen approach: Don't force the book. Open yourself to the story. Allow the story to flower.

5) Find a Writers Group to Join; Hire an Editor or Writing Coach to Help You With Your Book. New points of view can help you get unstuck. A solid critique from other writers or editors can open up your vision and expand your story-telling horizons. These people can also help you solve character and plot problems that stand in the way of your story.

6) Embrace Solitude.
There is comfort in being alone.
There is renewal in retreat.
This is where you refill the cup.
This is how a writer comes home.

7) Listen to the Silence. We all have voices that must be heeded, voices that must be heard. Not the negative voices that tell us what we cannot do, but the voices that tell us what we can do—that speak to us of our stories and our characters and our lives.

We cannot hear these voices if we fill our lives with noise.

Listen.

Listen to the silence.

8) Write. Write. Write anything. Writing enforces will. Write grocery lists or journal entries or essays. If you can't manage that, make lists of words. Favorite words. Angry words. Happy words. Silly words. Splendid words. Power words. If you can't write anything at all, copy. Copy stories by Margaret Wise Brown or poems by Shel Silverstein. Copy the opening paragraphs of your favorite books. Copy until you can write again: one line, two lines, one short sentence at a time. Write. Always write.

Afterthought

If you are stuck, focus on the immutable fact that nothing—neither darkness or light nor sorrow or joy—ever remains the same. Remind yourself that there are times in all our lives when we lose our daring. There are times when we lose our nerve. There are times when we live in fear of being found out and when putting words on the page is impossible. There are also times when we must wander in the wilderness in order to save ourselves. But this singular malady called writer's block is often no more than a momentary loss of will. Time repairs some things; determination restores others. Whatever the cause for your temporary lapse, there is a cure.

Patience. Intention. Tenacity. Fortitude. Spirit. Faith. Forgiveness. Breath. These qualities illuminate the dark times. And accentuate the light.

Believe.

CHAPTER TWENTY-ONE

The Care and Feeding of Your Creative Spirit

*We always know much more than we think we know—
otherwise we couldn't be writers.*

—Norman Mailer

THE BIRTHRIGHT

Creativity is a voracious animal. It needs to be fed regularly. If you leave it untended for too long, you run the risk of starving your passion and diminishing your spirit.

Most people think of creativity as a mystery, something that appears to us out of a magical mist. We either have it or we don't. Nothing could be further from the truth. Creativity is the gift that lifts us out of the ether and makes us human. The problem is, from early childhood, most of us are taught that imagination is inferior to intellect—that creativity is inferior to logic.

When my niece was two years old, one night she pointed to a wispy cloud drifting over the moon and exclaimed, "Look, Grandma! The moon is melting!"

Because the realities of life had not yet inhibited the purity of her imagination, that sweet child's vision was as luminous and fanciful as a poet's. And as original. Creativity is part of our essential nature. It is our birthright, a blessing connected with the most fundamental core of our being. And as such, it should not only be treated with kindness, it should be kindled and honored and treated with respect.

Nine Ways to Nourish the Creative Spirit

1) Read. Read. Read. For a writer, reading is the food that sustains the discipline. Read children's books. Read adult books. Read poetry and magazines and newspapers.

It isn't enough, however, merely to read. When I first began to write, I thought the fact I had read so many books would sustain me in my novice efforts. The problem was, I had never read a book with a consciousness of what the writer was doing; I had never noticed the technique behind the fiction. Therefore, when I began to construct my own story, I didn't know how to do it.

With that in mind, I suggest that if you want to learn how to write, you need to learn how to read in a way that will teach you how to write. As in so much of life, awareness is the key.

Questions to ask yourself as you read.

- How does the author open the story?

- How does the author indicate a shift in time?

- How does the author move from one place to another?

- How does the author introduce the hero?

- How are plot and subplot woven together?

- How does the hero evolve from beginning to end?

- How does the story move from beginning to middle to end?

- How is the villain portrayed?

- How does the author create tension?

- What are the obstacles the hero must overcome?

- How are different scenes opened?

- What is the Throughline of the book?

- How does language enhance the story?

- How are the voices of the characters differentiated?

- Why is the ending inevitable?

2) Explore the Arts. Art is not born in a vacuum. Movies, plays, art exhibits, concerts—all these events are drawn from the common well of creativity. Not only do they enrich one another, they improve one another.

Seeking out the creative experience of others opens our mind and our vision to new worlds. Just because a painting by Mark Rothko is abstract doesn't mean it can't speak to us about longing and spirituality. Whether it is a play about a dying parent, a film about a disaffected youth or a symphony about a heroic leader, the creative core of all these works can teach us about the creative spirit in our own lives.

3) Heed the Three Ds. Writing isn't a matter of sitting around and waiting for the spirit to move you. Writing requires desire, discipline and determination. That's not always easy when you have a full-time job, you have family problems or you're a parent struggling to make ends meet. But that's when you need the three Ds most.

• *Desire.* Most of us can't just toss off a book and expect it to sell. We not only have to entertain the notion of writing a book, we have to want to write it. And we have to want it enough to back up that desire with discipline and determination.

• *Discipline.* Discipline means we sit at the desk every day whether we are in the mood to write or not. Discipline means we honor the art by honing the craft. Discipline means if we don't feel well, or we are stuck or we have family obligations, we write anyway. Discipline means we make up our minds not to let ourselves down.

• *Determination.* When you're determined to do something, the first thing you learn is not to let obstacles bring you to a stop. This isn't to say that the best laid plans of mice and men don't sometimes go awry. We've all been waylaid by life. But the heart of determination is opening yourself to the experience at hand and learning how to roll with the punches.

• *My 3-D day.* I began my first book when my sons were six and eight years old. We lived in a small cottage, and the only place I had to write was a tiny table set near the back door where neighborhood children ran in and out of the house all day long.

I started writing the novel in the fall. By spring I had moved into the heart of the book and momentum was on my side. I was stoked, I was cooking, I was running on all eight cylinders.

One fine April morning I discovered both my boys had developed a condition that required I wash every item in the house they or we had touched. Sheets, towels, clothes. Everything that could be washed should be washed.

Between kids running back and forth past my desk, between fixing lunch and cleaning the kitchen, washing, folding and putting away seven loads of laundry, and supervising children all day long, I pounded out twenty pages on my Smith Corona portable.

On a good day with no interruptions, twenty pages would be a spectacular accomplishment. On this day, it was a miracle. I can only tell you I did it because I was driven by the 3-Ds I am now writing about twenty-four years and forty-two books after the fact.

4) Set goals. Successful writers set goals for themselves. Once they set those goals, they do everything in their power to stick to them. This discipline rests at the heart of the creative process.

It's important to be realistic about your goals. If you're working full time and you have two children to care for, setting a goal of writing three hours a day sets you up for daily defeat. It's all right to stretch yourself. It's not all right to stretch yourself beyond a sensible limit.

• *Time goals.* Some writers decide on a specific amount of time they are going to spend writing each day. Whether they can only manage half an hour or are able to devote eight hours a day to their craft as Dr. Seuss did, they sit themselves down at their desks and they stay there until that goal has been met.

This doesn't mean every moment of that time is going to be devoted exclusively to writing. But it does mean that the daily discipline of being there sets the standard for their craft.

• *Page goals.* If time spent at the desk doesn't feel right for you, set a minimum number of pages to write per day. Whether it's one or five or ten pages a day, set your goal and stick to it.

Writing a book brings out the restlessness in me. I get up and down from the desk a lot. I walk into the garden and check the flowers, dead-head the pansies, count the number of black and green striped caterpillars—soon to be Anise Swallowtail butterflies—feeding on my fennel. I go on errands, talk to friends and walk my dog. As a consequence, a time goal isn't effective for me.

When I am writing a book, I set my minimum at five pages a day.

This means whether I'm in the mood or not; whether I produce five pages and use every word, or produce five pages and throw every word away the next day, I must turn out those pages. No matter how late the hour or how exhausted I am, I don't leave the desk for the day until I have accomplished this goal.

5) Embrace the Process. I often look at writing as a process akin to having having a split personality. One part of me focuses on the goal. The other part focuses on where I am at any given moment.

I'm blessed. Even though I wrestle with prose, I love my work. I love the process of writing, the sound, the rhythm, the taste and texture of language. I love the way words roll around in my mind until they find their way home. Not all writers feel this way. As Red Smith once said, "Writing is easy. I just open a vein and bleed."

Whether you enjoy the process of writing or not, my advice is to make your peace with it. It is the process, not the goal, that gets you where you want to go.

6) Honor the Mystery and Magic. Whatever some people might say, there is a mystery and magic to writing. Not in how we get our creativity but how we use it. There is an element of surprise, of ideas appearing out of nowhere and connections leaping out of dreams, that cannot be accounted for in the daily living of our lives. Call it woo-woo. Call it inspiration. Call it synthesis. Call it whatever you wish. This magical and mysterious element of the creative process does exist. To ignore it is to put your book and your creative life at risk.

7) Seek the Universal. The reason certain books resonate with readers is because they touch on universal themes. However, these themes are not created at a universal level. They are grounded in the particular experience of a particular person at a particular moment in time.

Harry Potter appeals to a massive audience not because he's a beguiling orphan buffeted by fate. His personal appeal lies in the fact that he touches on our innate relationship with sadness and loss and how we deal with these personal demons. Harry's universality is rooted in the fact that he evokes the deep and undeniable longing to transform our lives that we all carry close to our hearts.

8) Daydream. As children, most of us were admonished to pay attention to the task at hand and—for goodness sake—stop daydreaming! What a disservice this message conveys to children. Vision and fantasy, creativity and imagination, live at the heart of daydreams. Welcome day-dreams into your life. They are gifts to be treasured, not dismissed.

9) *Dare.* Experiment. Combine unexpected elements. Play with words. Break the rules. Seek out the laughter in desperation and the humor in pain. Writing is a risk—take the dare.

MUSINGS ABOUT THE MUSE

In Greek mythology, the traditional Muses are the nine daughters of Zeus that preside over the arts and sciences. The Greeks also honored three earlier Muses dedicated to Meditation, Remembrance and Song. In my personal mythology, I believe we are all born with a Muse. The problem is, most of us have it "civilized" out of us before the age of seven. Either that, or we ignore this gift for so long that it dies of disinterest and neglect.

We all struggle to achieve a measure of worldly success. But in the process of this struggle, many of us forget how to honor the creative force within.

Some people invoke this part of themselves through prayer, others through meditation. Others reach this goal through becoming involved in an absorbing activity such as running, gardening, sewing, cooking, Tai Chi or carpentry. However you get there, you can welcome the fanciful and the unusual into your life by continuing to seek new ways to elevate your spirit and celebrate your imagination.

Just in case all this Muse talk is making you nervous, I'm going to up the woo-woo ante and add the following instructions.

The Care and Feeding of the Muse

Don't Mess With the Muse. Don't delude yourself. You need the Muse more than she needs you. Therefore, if your Muse appears to have gone on vacation, I suggest persuasion instead of threats. Entice her into your life with gentle exercises. Close your eyes. Breathe deeply. Meditate. Daydream. Pray.

Never Take the Muse for Granted. Unconditional love isn't part of the spiritual vocabulary of the Muse. Just because you've been cruising down the creative road on automatic pilot, don't assume the Muse will always be sitting next to you in the passenger seat. She's temperamental. She's cranky. Like any other being, she needs to be acknowledged regularly. If you don't pay attention to her, she's likely to jump out of the car the first time you come to a stoplight.

Trust the Muse. Believe. It's not always easy to trust the path that's been laid out before you. Even though you're filled with fear, if your calling is to write, honor that calling. Creative courage isn't won overnight, but the prize is worth the effort.

Remember to Thank the Muse. If someone is doing something for you every day, good manners suggest that you thank that person. Same with the Muse. You express your gratitude by staying open to the creative leap, by meditating and remembering, by being receptive to new ideas and welcoming fresh ways of thinking. You also do this by behaving as though the Muse exists and thanking her every morning for her presence in your life and for her contributions to your art.

Afterword

Nothing in the world can take the place of persistence.
Talent will not; nothing is more common than unsuccessful men with talent.
Genius will not; unrecorded genius is almost a proverb.
Education will not; the world is full of educated derelicts.
Persistence and determination alone are omnipotent.

—Calvin Coolidge

We all walk the wire when we sit down in front of a blank page or an empty computer screen. We all work without a net. Sometimes it's hard to find our balance. Sometimes it's hard to recover from a fall. Sometimes it's hard to bear the loneliness or disappointment. And sometimes it's hard to find the strength to begin or the courage to believe. But with attention and focus and determination, it is possible for us to complete that long and scary journey to the other side.

How do we do this? One foot in front of another. One step at a time.

One word in front of another.

One sentence at a time.

Here.

Now.

Take a deep breath.

Step off the edge.

And begin.

The End

Reading List

Whether you're a novice or a published author, reading books about writing can open up new worlds and give rise to new ideas. These books can also offer you comfort when you're stuck and show you new ways to approach old problems.

Sometimes you need a plain how-to book. Other times you need a philosophical insight to the craft. Whatever your preference, you'll find it on this list.

Bird by Bird by Anne Lamott

The Writing Life by Annie Dillard

The Art of Writing for Children by Connie C. Epstein

Writing for Children and Teenagers by Lee Wyndham

How to Write and Sell Children's Picture Books by Jean E. Karl

You Can Write Children's Books by Tracey E. Dils

Scene and Structure by Jack M. Bickham

How to Write a Damn Good Novel by James N. Frey

How to Write a Damn Good Novel, II by James N. Frey

Building Better Plots by Robert Kernen

Beginnings, Middles & Ends by Nancy Kress

Creating Characters Kids Will Love by Elaine Marie Alphin

Story Sparkers: A Creative Guide for Children's Writers by Marcia Thornton Jones and Debbie Dadey

Touchstone Books

You may have noticed that there are several children's books I have referred to over and over again in the writing of this book. I call them my Touchstone Books—those books that not only exemplify good writing but have lasted throughout the years. Here my list of suggestions. Edit it. Add to it. But most of all, read the books.

Where the Wild Things Are by Maurice Sendak

The Catcher in the Rye by J.D. Salinger

Bridge to Terabithia by Katherine Paterson

The Runaway Bunny by Margaret Wise Brown

A Separate Peace by John Knowles

The Outsiders by S.E. Hinton

The Little Prince by Antoine de Saint-Exupery

Charlotte's Web by E.B. White

Slugs by David Greenberg

Maniac Magee by Jerry Spinelli

The Golden Compass by Philip Pullman

Index